the hummingbird bakery

cookbook

the hummingbird bakery
cookbook

Tarek Malouf and The Hummingbird Bakers

photography by Peter Cassidy

RYLAND
PETERS
& SMALL

LONDON NEW YORK

Design, Photographic Art Direction,
and Prop Styling Steve Painter
Senior Editor Céline Hughes
Production Manager Patricia Harrington
Art Director Leslie Harrington
Publishing Director Alison Starling

Food Stylist Bridget Sargeson
Indexer Hilary Bird

Hummingbird Bakery corporate branding
and company graphic design Sue Thedens
Illustrations Debbie Adamson

First published in the US in 2009
by Ryland Peters & Small, Inc.
519 Broadway, 5th Floor
New York, NY 10012
www.rylandpeters.com

10 9 8 7 6

ISBN: 978 1 84597 831 0

Library of Congress Cataloging-in-Publication Data

Malouf, Tarek.
    The Hummingbird Bakery cookbook / Tarek Malouf
and The Hummingbird bakers ; photography by
Peter Cassidy.
        p. cm.
    Includes index.
    ISBN 978-1-84597-831-0
    1. Baking. 2. Desserts. 3. Hummingbird Bakery.
I. Title.
    TX761.M27 2009
    641.8'15--dc22

2008049309

Notes
- All spoon measurements are level, unless
otherwise specified.
- All eggs are medium, unless otherwise specified.
Uncooked or partially cooked eggs should not be
served to the very young, the very old, those with
compromised immune systems, or to pregnant
women.
- Ovens should be preheated to the specified
temperature. Recipes in this book were tested
using a regular oven. If using a convection oven,
follow the manufacturer's instructions for adjusting
temperatures.

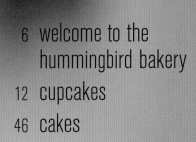

contents

Welcome to The Hummingbird Bakery

I first thought about opening The Hummingbird Bakery after spending Thanksgiving with cousins in North Carolina. After eating too much pecan pie, banana cream pie, and apple pie, I wondered why there wasn't a place in London that made these types of desserts to a high standard. On subsequent trips to the USA, and New York in particular, I visited various bakeries that made all the goodies that I enjoyed eating, especially cupcakes. And at that point, cupcakes seemed to be unknown in London—at least, they were hard to buy.

I started planning the bakery in 2002. First, I attended baking classes in New York so that I would understand the ingredients and techniques used in American baking. Then came the fun task of devising recipes and testing them on friends and family. I always had an idea of which core cakes I wanted to sell—and for these I tested and tweaked many, many recipes until I found what I thought tasted the most authentic. I even held parties for friends so that they could test the recipes and tell me if I was getting them right.

The next important step was finding the perfect site for the first shop. I felt it should be a place that was relatively busy, with a bohemian feel. A unit in Portobello Road in London's Notting Hill came up by chance and I immediately jumped on it. It proved to be heaven-sent because as soon as the shop opened, a lot of high-profile customers began to write and speak about it. On Saturdays, when the famous market is on, tourists flock to Portobello and they were soon queueing up to try our cupcakes. During the quieter weekdays, the publicity surrounding the Bakery kept it busy. Soon, recommendations were appearing on blogs, and friends were being urged to try our cupcakes when they visited London. Now, thanks to the success of our first branch, we also have a shop in South Kensington.

It will probably come as no surprise that we sell far more cupcakes than anything else. They seem to be popular because of their cute size, the childhood memories they evoke, and their sheer versatility. Our best-selling cupcakes are vanilla with pink frosting, which reflects our female-dominated customer base, and red velvet, simply because they look and taste so distinctive. For many people, layer-cakes are essential for birthdays. Besides the red velvet and vanilla, our carrot cake is extremely popular. Decorating a three-layer cake takes time but the result is worth the effort! Pies are such an American tradition, especially for festive occasions. Our customers love lemon meringue and Key lime pies the most—the fluffy meringue and whipped cream toppings are so beautiful and mouthwatering that they never last long in the shop. Other treats such as muffins, cookies, and bars were always favorites in school lunchboxes when I was at school. Our brownies are extremely popular, so we developed three versions: plain (no nuts), frosted (more cakey with nuts and frosting), and my favorite, brownies topped with baked cheesecake and raspberry whipped cream!

I'm so pleased to share my favorite cakes with you in this book. I hope you enjoy baking them as much we all do at The Hummingbird Bakery.

Tarek Malouf

frostings

These frostings make enough to frost 12 cupcakes. To cover a cake (top and sides), double the recipes. They are used in cupcake and cake recipes throughout the book. Tint the Vanilla or Cream Cheese frostings any shade you like with a couple of drops of food coloring mixed in until evenly incorporated. At the Hummingbird, we like our cupcake frostings in pretty candy colors, but you can choose any color you like.

vanilla

2 cups confectioners' sugar, sifted

5 tablespoons unsalted butter, at room temperature

2 tablespoons whole milk

a couple of drops of pure vanilla extract

Makes enough to frost 12 cupcakes (double the recipe for 8-inch cake)

Beat the confectioners' sugar and butter together in a freestanding electric mixer with a paddle attachment on medium-slow speed until the mixture comes together and is well mixed. Turn the mixer down to a slower speed. Combine the milk and vanilla in a separate bowl, then add to the butter mixture a couple of teaspoons at a time. Once all the milk has been incorporated, turn the mixer up to high speed. Continue beating until the frosting is light and fluffy, at least 5 minutes. The longer the frosting is beaten, the fluffier and lighter it becomes.

chocolate

2⅓ cups confectioners' sugar, sifted

6½ tablespoons unsalted butter, at room temperature

⅓ cup unsweetened cocoa powder, sifted

2 tablespoons whole milk

Makes enough to frost 12 cupcakes (double the recipe for 8-inch cake)

Beat the confectioners' sugar, butter, and cocoa together in a freestanding electric mixer with a paddle attachment on medium-slow speed until the mixture comes together and is well mixed. Turn the mixer down to a slower speed. Add the milk to the butter mixture a couple of teaspoons at a time. Once all the milk has been incorporated, turn the mixer up to high speed. Continue beating until the frosting is light and fluffy, about 5 minutes. The longer the frosting is beaten, the fluffier and lighter it becomes.

cream cheese

2⅓ cups confectioners' sugar, sifted

3 tablespoons unsalted butter, at room temperature

4 oz. cream cheese, cold

Makes enough to frost 12 cupcakes (double the recipe for 8-inch cake)

Beat the confectioners' sugar and butter together in a freestanding electric mixer with a paddle attachment on medium-slow speed until the mixture comes together and is well mixed. Add the cream cheese in one go and beat until it is completely incorporated. Turn the mixer up to medium-high speed. Continue beating until the frosting is light and fluffy, at least 5 minutes. Do not overbeat, as it can quickly become runny.

cupcakes

vanilla cupcakes

Our vanilla cupcakes, topped with candy-colored Vanilla Frosting and sprinkles, are what the Hummingbird Bakery is best known for, and they never fail to please. When you make these at home, don't overbake them—they should be light golden and spring back when touched. This way you will ensure an airy, moist cake with a subtle vanilla taste. The cupcakes can also be topped with Chocolate Frosting (see page 11).

1 cup all-purpose flour

a scant ¾ cup sugar

1½ teaspoons baking powder

a pinch of salt

3 tablespoons unsalted butter, at room temperature

½ cup whole milk

1 egg

¼ teaspoon pure vanilla extract

1 quantity Vanilla Frosting (page 11)

nonpareils or other edible sprinkles, to decorate

a 12-hole cupcake pan, lined with paper cases

Makes 12

Preheat the oven to 325°F.

Put the flour, sugar, baking powder, salt, and butter in a freestanding electric mixer with a paddle attachment (or use a handheld electric whisk) and beat on slow speed until you get a sandy consistency and everything is combined. Gradually pour in half the milk and beat until the milk is just incorporated.

Whisk the egg, vanilla, and remaining milk together in a separate bowl for a few seconds, then pour into the flour mixture and continue beating until just incorporated (scrape any unmixed ingredients from the side of the bowl with a rubber spatula). Continue mixing for a couple more minutes until the batter is smooth. Do not overmix.

Spoon the batter into the paper cases until two-thirds full and bake in the preheated oven for 20–25 minutes, or until light golden and the cake bounces back when touched. A skewer inserted in the center should come out clean. Let the cupcakes cool slightly in the pan before turning out onto a wire rack to cool completely.

When the cupcakes are cold, spoon the Vanilla Frosting on top and decorate with nonpareils.

chocolate cupcakes

We use a devil's food cake for our chocolate base. The cocoa powder gives the cake a dark color and chocolatey kick. The cake should be light and moist, with all the ingredients well incorporated. But don't overbeat the batter, as the cake will be too heavy. For chocolate lovers, top with Chocolate Frosting (see page 11). For a more restrained option, both the Vanilla and Cream Cheese Frostings work well.

¾ cup plus 2 tablespoons all-purpose flour

2½ tablespoons unsweetened cocoa powder

a scant ¾ cup sugar

1½ teaspoons baking powder

a pinch of salt

3 tablespoons unsalted butter, at room temperature

½ cup whole milk

1 egg

¼ teaspoon pure vanilla extract

1 quantity Chocolate, Vanilla, or Cream Cheese Frosting (page 11)

chocolate jimmies or edible balls, to decorate

a 12-hole cupcake pan, lined with paper cases

Makes 12

Preheat the oven to 325°F.

Put the flour, cocoa, sugar, baking powder, salt, and butter in a freestanding electric mixer with a paddle attachment (or use a handheld electric whisk) and beat on slow speed until you get a sandy consistency and everything is combined.

Whisk the milk, egg, and vanilla together in a pitcher, then slowly pour about half into the flour mixture, beat to combine, and turn the mixer up to high speed to get rid of any lumps.

Turn the mixer down to a slower speed and slowly pour in the remaining milk mixture (scrape any unmixed ingredients from the side of the bowl with a rubber spatula). Continue mixing for a couple more minutes until the batter is smooth but do not overmix.

Spoon the batter into the paper cases until two-thirds full and bake in the preheated oven for 20–25 minutes, or until the cake bounces back when touched. A skewer inserted in the center should come out clean. Let the cupcakes cool slightly in the pan before turning out onto a wire rack to cool completely.

When the cupcakes are cold, spoon the Chocolate, Vanilla, or Cream Cheese Frosting on top and decorate with chocolate jimmies or edible balls.

red velvet cupcakes

It seems people can't resist the red velvet cupcakes' deep red crumb with white Cream Cheese Frosting. Mix all the ingredients well so that the sponge has an even color and texture. For added color contrast, you can sprinkle some extra red velvet cake crumbs over the frosted cupcakes. To make a red velvet cake instead, double the quantities below, divide between three 8-inch cake pans and bake for 25 minutes at the same oven temperature. Frost with 2 quantities of Cream Cheese Frosting.

4 tablespoons unsalted butter, at room temperature

¾ cup sugar

1 egg

1 tablespoon unsweetened cocoa powder

2 tablespoons red food coloring

½ teaspoon pure vanilla extract

½ cup buttermilk

1 cup plus 2 tablespoons all-purpose flour

½ teaspoon salt

½ teaspoon baking soda

1½ teaspoons distilled white vinegar

1 quantity Cream Cheese Frosting (page 11)

a 12-hole cupcake pan, lined with paper cases

Makes 12

Preheat the oven to 325°F.

Put the butter and the sugar in a freestanding electric mixer with a paddle attachment (or use a handheld electric whisk) and beat on medium speed until light and fluffy and well mixed. Turn the mixer up to high speed, slowly add the egg, and beat until everything is well incorporated.

In a separate bowl, mix together the cocoa, red food coloring, and vanilla to make a thick, dark paste. Add to the butter mixture and mix thoroughly until evenly combined and colored (scrape any unmixed ingredients from the side of the bowl with a rubber spatula). Turn the mixer down to slow speed and slowly pour in half the buttermilk. Beat until well mixed, then add half the flour and beat until everything is well incorporated. Repeat this process until all the buttermilk and flour have been added. Scrape down the side of the bowl again. Turn the mixer up to high speed and beat until you have a smooth, even batter. Turn the mixer down to low speed and add the salt, baking soda, and vinegar. Beat until well mixed, then turn up the speed again and beat for a couple more minutes.

Spoon the batter into the paper cases until two-thirds full and bake in the preheated oven for 20–25 minutes, or until the cake bounces back when touched. A skewer inserted in the center should come out clean. Let the cupcakes cool slightly in the pan before turning out onto a wire rack to cool completely.

When the cupcakes are cold, spoon the Cream Cheese Frosting on top.

See photographs on pages 18 and 19.

lemon cupcakes

Hollowing out a bit of the cake and putting in a small spoonful of lemon curd makes this cupcake very moist and tangy. Lemon is always a popular alternative to chocolate or vanilla desserts. The trick is to keep the frosting slightly tart, to temper the sugar.

1 cup all-purpose flour

¾ cup sugar

1½ teaspoons baking powder

2 tablespoons grated lemon zest, plus extra to decorate

3 tablespoons unsalted butter, at room temperature

½ cup whole milk

1 egg

lemon frosting

2 cups confectioners' sugar, sifted

5 tablespoons unsalted butter, at room temperature

2 tablespoons grated lemon zest

a couple of drops of yellow food coloring (optional)

2 tablespoons whole milk

a 12-hole cupcake pan, lined with paper cases

Makes 12

Preheat the oven to 325°F.

Put the flour, sugar, baking powder, lemon zest, and butter in a freestanding electric mixer with a paddle attachment (or use a handheld electric whisk) and beat on slow speed until you get a sandy consistency and everything is combined. Gradually pour in the milk and beat until just incorporated.

Add the egg to the flour mixture and continue beating until just incorporated (scrape any unmixed ingredients from the side of the bowl with a rubber spatula). Continue mixing for a couple more minutes until the batter is smooth. Do not overmix.

Spoon the batter into the paper cases until two-thirds full and bake in the preheated oven for 20–25 minutes, or until the cake bounces back when touched. A skewer inserted in the center should come out clean. Let the cupcakes cool slightly in the pan before turning out onto a wire rack to cool completely.

For the lemon frosting: Beat together the confectioners' sugar, butter, lemon zest, and food coloring, if using, in a freestanding electric mixer with a paddle attachment (or use a handheld electric whisk) on medium-slow speed until the mixture comes together and is well mixed. Turn the mixer down to a slower speed. Slowly pour in the milk, then when it is all incorporated, turn the mixer up to high speed. Continue beating until the frosting is light and fluffy, at least 5 minutes. The longer the frosting is beaten, the fluffier and lighter it becomes.

When the cupcakes are cold, spoon the lemon frosting on top and decorate with a little lemon zest.

strawberry cheesecake cupcakes

It's important to use pieces of fresh strawberry in this recipe—they moisten the cake and texture of the cupcakes. The crumbled cookies sprinkled on top add the flavor of a cheesecake base. At the Bakery we like to cover the frosting generously with crumbled cookies but you can add as little or as much as you like.

1 cup all-purpose flour

a scant ¾ cup sugar

1½ teaspoons baking powder

a pinch of salt

3 tablespoons unsalted butter, at room temperature

½ cup whole milk

½ teaspoon pure vanilla extract

1 egg

12 large strawberries, chopped into small pieces

3–6 oz. wholemeal cookies, such as English digestives or graham crackers

1 quantity Cream Cheese Frosting (page 11)

a 12-hole cupcake pan, lined with paper cases

Makes 12

Preheat the oven to 325°F.

Put the flour, sugar, baking powder, salt, and butter in a freestanding electric mixer with a paddle attachment (or use a handheld electric whisk) and beat on slow speed until you get a sandy consistency and everything is combined.

Pour in the milk and vanilla and beat on medium speed until all the ingredients are well mixed (scrape any unmixed ingredients from the side of the bowl with a rubber spatula). Add the egg and beat well for a few minutes to ensure the ingredients are well incorporated.

Divide the chopped strawberries between the paper cases. Spoon the batter on top until two-thirds full and bake in the preheated oven for 20–25 minutes, or until light golden and the cake bounces back when touched. A skewer inserted in the center should come out clean. Let the cupcakes cool slightly in the pan before turning out onto a wire rack to cool completely.

Roughly break up the cookies or crackers and put them in a food processor. Process until finely ground. When the cupcakes are cold, spoon the Cream Cheese Frosting on top and finish with a sprinkling of ground cookies.

black bottom cupcakes

The black bottom cupcake looks innocent, but packs a punch! A dark chocolate cake with a dollop of cheesecake baked into it, we top ours with Cream Cheese Frosting for extra impact. The chocolate base is different from our normal chocolate cupcakes—it's darker, slightly less sweet, and marries well with the cheesecake center. Omit the cream cheese frosting for a more moderate treat.

1 quantity Cream Cheese Frosting (page 11) (optional)

chocolate cake base

1½ cups all-purpose flour

½ cup plus 1 tablespoon sugar

⅓ cup unsweetened cocoa powder, plus extra to decorate

½ teaspoon baking soda

¼ cup sunflower oil

1½ teaspoons distilled white vinegar

½ teaspoon pure vanilla extract

cheesecake filling

4½ oz. cream cheese

⅓ cup sugar

1 egg

½ teaspoon pure vanilla extract

a pinch of salt

⅔ cup chocolate chips

a 12-hole cupcake pan, lined with paper cases

Makes 12

Preheat the oven to 325°F.

For the chocolate cake base: Put the flour, sugar, cocoa, and baking soda in a large bowl and mix with a handheld electric whisk on slow speed until all the dry ingredients are well incorporated.

Put the oil, vinegar, vanilla, and ½ cup water in a glass and whisk to combine. While the electric whisk is running in the flour bowl, slowly add the oil mixture, increasing the speed of the blender as the mixture thickens. Continue to beat until all the ingredients are incorporated (scrape any unmixed ingredients from the side of the bowl with a rubber spatula).

Spoon the batter into the paper cases and set aside.

For the cheesecake filling: Beat together the cream cheese, sugar, egg, vanilla, and salt in a freestanding electric mixer with a paddle attachment (or use a handheld electric whisk) on medium-slow speed until smooth and fluffy.

Stir in the chocolate chips by hand until evenly dispersed. Don't overmix, otherwise the cream cheese will start to split.

Scoop about 1 tablespoon of the cheesecake filling on top of the cupcake batter in the cases and bake in the preheated oven for about 20 minutes, or until the cupcakes are firm to the touch and they have an even golden color on the cheesecake filling. Don't overbake as the cheesecake will become very dry and crumbly. Let the cupcakes cool slightly in the pan before turning out onto a wire rack to cool completely.

When the cupcakes are cold, spoon the Cream Cheese Frosting on top, if using, and decorate with a light sprinkling of cocoa.

lavender cupcakes

Many people can't imagine eating a lavender-infused cake, but this flavor is very popular in the summer. Infusing the milk with lavender flowers makes the flavor subtle. The frosting can be left plain, or you can use a bit of food coloring to give it a light lavender color.

½ cup whole milk

3 tablespoons dried lavender flowers

1 cup all-purpose flour

a scant ¾ cup sugar

1½ teaspoons baking powder

3 tablespoons unsalted butter, at room temperature

1 egg

12 small sprigs of lavender (optional)

lavender frosting

2 tablespoons whole milk

1 tablespoon dried lavender flowers

2 cups confectioners' sugar, sifted

5 tablespoons unsalted butter, at room temperature

a couple of drops of purple food coloring (optional)

a 12-hole cupcake pan, lined with paper cases

Makes 12

Put the milk and dried lavender flowers in a measuring cup, cover, and refrigerate for a few hours, or overnight if possible. Do the same with the milk and lavender flowers for the frosting, in a separate cup.

Preheat the oven to 325°F.

Put the flour, sugar, baking powder, and butter in a freestanding electric mixer with a paddle attachment (or use a handheld electric whisk) and beat on slow speed until you get a sandy consistency and everything is combined.

Strain the lavender-infused milk (for the cupcake) and slowly pour into the flour mixture, beating well until all the ingredients are well mixed. Add the egg and beat well (scrape any unmixed ingredients from the side of the bowl with a rubber spatula).

Spoon the batter into the paper cases until two-thirds full and bake in the preheated oven for 20–25 minutes, or until the cake bounces back when touched. A skewer inserted in the center should come out clean. Let the cupcakes cool slightly in the pan before turning out onto a wire rack to cool completely.

For the lavender frosting: Beat together the confectioners' sugar, butter, and food coloring, if using, in a freestanding electric mixer with a paddle attachment (or use a handheld electric whisk) on medium-slow speed until the mixture comes together and is well mixed. Turn the mixer down to slow speed. Strain the lavender-infused milk and slowly pour into the butter mixture. Once all the milk is incorporated, turn the mixer up to high speed. Continue beating until the frosting is light and fluffy, at least 5 minutes. The longer the frosting is beaten, the fluffier and lighter it becomes.

When the cupcakes are cold, spoon the lavender frosting on top and decorate with a sprig of lavender, if using.

hazelnut and chocolate cupcakes

Sometimes chocolate alone just won't do, which is why we've added irresistible hazelnut chocolate spread to these cupcakes. Decorate with hazelnuts for extra crunch.

¾ cup plus 1 tablespoon all-purpose flour

2½ tablespoons unsweetened cocoa powder

a scant ¾ cup sugar

1½ teaspoons baking powder

a pinch of salt

3 tablespoons butter, at room temperature

½ cup whole milk

1 egg

½ cup hazelnut and chocolate spread (such as Nutella)

about 36 whole, shelled hazelnuts, to decorate

hazelnut and chocolate frosting

2 cups confectioners' sugar, sifted

5 tablespoons unsalted butter, at room temperature

2 tablespoons whole milk

⅓ cup hazelnut and chocolate spread (such as Nutella)

a 12-hole cupcake pan, lined with paper cases

Makes 12

Preheat the oven to 325°F.

Put the flour, cocoa, sugar, baking powder, salt, and butter in a freestanding electric mixer with a paddle attachment (or use a handheld electric whisk) and beat on slow speed until you get a sandy consistency and everything is combined.

Slowly pour the milk into the flour mixture, beating well until all the ingredients are well mixed. Add the egg and beat well (scrape any unmixed ingredients from the side of the bowl with a rubber spatula).

Spoon the batter into the paper cases until two-thirds full and bake in the preheated oven for about 20 minutes, or until the cake bounces back when touched. Let the cupcakes cool slightly in the pan before turning out onto a wire rack to cool completely.

When the cupcakes are cold, hollow out a small section in the center of each one and fill with a dollop of hazelnut and chocolate spread.

For the hazelnut and chocolate frosting: Beat the confectioners' sugar and butter together in a freestanding electric mixer with a paddle attachment (or use a handheld electric whisk) on medium-slow speed until the mixture comes together and is well mixed. Turn the mixer down to a slower speed. Slowly pour in the milk, then when it is all incorporated, turn the mixer up to high speed. Continue beating until the frosting is light and fluffy, at least 5 minutes. The longer the frosting is beaten, the fluffier and lighter it becomes.

Stir in the hazelnut and chocolate spread by hand until evenly mixed into the frosting. When the cupcakes are cold, spoon the frosting on top and finish with about 3 hazelnuts per cupcake.

coconut and pineapple cupcakes

Coconut and pineapple give these cupcakes a tropical flavor. Grated fresh coconut can be used instead of desiccated coconut for an even better flavor.

1 cup all-purpose flour

a scant ¾ cup sugar

1½ teaspoons baking powder

a pinch of salt

3 tablespoons unsalted butter, at room temperature

½ cup coconut milk

½ teaspoon pure vanilla extract

1 egg

9 canned pineapple rings, chopped into small pieces

desiccated coconut, to decorate

coconut frosting

2 cups confectioners' sugar, sifted

5 tablespoons unsalted butter, at room temperature

2 tablespoons coconut milk

a 12-hole cupcake pan, lined with paper cases

Makes 12

Preheat the oven to 325°F.

Put the flour, sugar, baking powder, salt, and butter in a freestanding electric mixer with a paddle attachment (or use a handheld electric whisk) and beat on slow speed until you get a sandy consistency and everything is combined.

Mix the coconut milk and vanilla in a separate bowl, then beat into the flour mixture on medium speed until well combined. Add the egg and beat well (scrape any unmixed ingredients from the side of the bowl with a rubber spatula).

Divide the chopped pineapple between the paper cases. Spoon the cupcake batter on top until two-thirds full and bake in the preheated oven for 20–25 minutes, or until light golden and the cake bounces back when touched. A skewer inserted in the center should come out clean. Let the cupcakes cool slightly in the pan before turning out onto a wire rack to cool completely.

For the coconut frosting: Beat the confectioners' sugar and butter together in a freestanding electric mixer with a paddle attachment (or use a handheld electric whisk) on medium-slow speed until the mixture comes together and is well mixed. Turn the mixer down to a slower speed and slowly pour in the coconut milk. Once all the milk has been incorporated, turn the mixer up to high speed. Continue beating until the frosting is very white, light, and fluffy, 5–10 minutes.

When the cupcakes are cold, spoon the coconut frosting on top and finish with a sprinkling of desiccated coconut.

banana and chocolate cupcakes

Bananas work so well when used in baking, as they become almost caramel-like when they cook. Chocolate Frosting works particularly well with these, but Vanilla or Cream Cheese (see page 11) can also be used.

1 cup all-purpose plain flour

a scant ¾ cup sugar

1 tablespoon baking powder

1 teaspoon ground cinnamon

1 teaspoon ground ginger

a pinch of salt

5 tablespoons unsalted butter, at room temperature

½ cup whole milk

2 eggs

1 ripe banana, peeled and mashed

1 quantity Chocolate Frosting (page 11)

1½ oz. bittersweet chocolate, grated with a cheese grater into shavings

a 12-hole cupcake pan, lined with paper cases

Makes 12

Preheat the oven to 325°F.

Put the flour, sugar, baking powder, cinnamon, ginger, salt, and butter in a freestanding electric mixer with a paddle attachment (or use a handheld electric whisk) and beat on slow speed until you get a sandy consistency and everything is combined.

Slowly pour the milk into the flour mixture, beating well until all the ingredients are well mixed. Add the eggs and beat well (scrape any unmixed ingredients from the side of the bowl with a rubber spatula).

Stir in the mashed banana by hand until evenly dispersed.

Spoon the batter into the paper cases until two-thirds full and bake in the preheated oven for about 20 minutes, or until light golden and the cake bounces back when touched. Let the cupcakes cool slightly in the pan before turning out onto a wire rack to cool completely.

When the cupcakes are cold, spoon the Chocolate Frosting on top and finish with the chocolate shavings.

green tea cupcakes

Green tea-flavored desserts are very popular in Japan. Green tea works so well in cakes, combined with either vanilla or chocolate. It's important to use green tea powder called 'Matcha'. Buy it from tea shops and specialty Asian supermarkets.

½ cup whole milk

3 green tea bags

¾ cup plus 1 tablespoon all-purpose flour

2½ tablespoons unsweetened cocoa powder

a scant ¾ cup sugar

1½ teaspoons baking powder

a pinch of salt

3 tablespoons unsalted butter, at room temperature

1 egg

¼ teaspoon pure vanilla extract

green tea frosting

2 cups confectioners' sugar, sifted

5 tablespoons unsalted butter, at room temperature

2½ tablespoons Matcha green tea powder, plus extra to decorate

2 tablespoons whole milk

a 12-hole cupcake pan, lined with paper cases

Makes 12

Put the milk and green tea bags in a measuring cup, cover, and refrigerate for a few hours, or overnight if possible.

Preheat the oven to 325°F.

Put the flour, cocoa, sugar, baking powder, salt, and butter in a freestanding electric mixer with a paddle attachment (or use a handheld electric whisk) and beat on slow speed until you get a sandy consistency and everything is combined.

Remove the green tea bags from the infused milk and combine with the egg and vanilla. Slowly pour half into the flour mixture, beating well until all the ingredients are well mixed. Turn the mixer up to high speed and beat well to make sure there are no lumps. Turn the speed down to medium-slow and slowly pour in the remaining milk mixture (scrape any unmixed ingredients from the side of the bowl with a rubber spatula). Continue mixing for a couple more minutes until the batter is smooth.

Spoon the batter into the paper cases until two-thirds full and bake in the preheated oven for 20–25 minutes, or until the cake bounces back when touched. A skewer inserted in the center should come out clean. Let the cupcakes cool slightly in the pan before turning out onto a wire rack to cool completely.

For the green tea frosting: Beat together the confectioners' sugar, butter, and Matcha powder in a freestanding electric mixer with a paddle attachment (or use a handheld electric whisk) on medium-slow speed until the mixture comes together and is well mixed. Turn the mixer down to a slower speed. Slowly pour in the milk, then when it is all incorporated, turn the mixer up to high speed. Continue beating until the frosting is light and fluffy, at least 5 minutes.

When the cupcakes are cold, spoon the frosting on top and decorate with a light sprinkling of Matcha powder.

peaches and cream cupcakes

A classic summer combination—using fresh peaches makes the recipe work so much better. Other fruits in season could be substituted.

1 cup all-purpose flour

a scant ¾ sugar

1½ teaspoons baking powder

a pinch of salt

3 tablespoons unsalted butter, at room temperature

½ cup whole milk

1 egg

¼ teaspoon pure vanilla extract

14 oz. canned peaches, sliced

1 quantity Vanilla Frosting (page 11)

light brown sugar, to decorate (optional)

a 12-hole cupcake pan, lined with paper cases

Makes 12

Preheat the oven to 325°F.

Put the flour, sugar, baking powder, salt, and butter in a freestanding electric mixer with a paddle attachment (or use a handheld electric whisk) and beat on slow speed until you get a sandy consistency and everything is combined. Gradually pour in half the milk and beat until the milk is just incorporated.

Whisk the egg, vanilla, and remaining milk together in a separate bowl for a few seconds, then pour into the flour mixture and continue beating until just incorporated (scrape any unmixed ingredients from the side of the bowl with a rubber spatula). Continue mixing for a couple more minutes until the batter is smooth. Do not overmix.

Divide the sliced peaches between the paper cases so that the base of each case is covered. Spoon the cupcake batter on top until two-thirds full and bake in the preheated oven for 20–25 minutes, or until light golden and the cake bounces back when touched. A skewer inserted in the center should come out clean. Let the cupcakes cool slightly in the pan before turning out onto a wire rack to cool completely.

When the cupcakes are cold, spoon the Vanilla Frosting on top and finish with a light sprinkling of light brown sugar, if using.

pumpkin cupcakes

These cupcakes are popular at Halloween and Thanksgiving. The light sprinkling of cinnamon over the Cream Cheese Frosting gives them a pretty finish.

1 cup all-purpose flour

a scant ¾ cup sugar

1 tablespoon baking powder

1½ teaspoons ground cinnamon, plus extra to decorate

a pinch of salt

3 tablespoons unsalted butter, at room temperature

½ cup whole milk

2 eggs

6½ oz. canned pumpkin purée

1 quantity Cream Cheese Frosting (page 11)

a 12-hole cupcake pan, lined with paper cases

Makes 12

Preheat the oven to 325°F.

Put the flour, sugar, baking powder, cinnamon, salt, and butter in a freestanding electric mixer with a paddle attachment (or use a handheld electric whisk) and beat on slow speed until you get a sandy consistency and everything is combined. Gradually pour in the milk and beat until well mixed.

Add the eggs to the mix and beat well (scrape any unmixed ingredients from the side of the bowl with a rubber spatula). Stir in the pumpkin purée by hand until evenly dispersed.

Spoon the batter into the paper cases until two-thirds full and bake in the preheated oven for about 20 minutes, or until light golden and the cake bounces back when touched. Let the cupcakes cool slightly in the pan before turning out onto a wire rack to cool completely.

When the cupcakes are cold, spoon the Cream Cheese Frosting on top and finish with a light sprinkling of cinnamon.

marshmallow cupcakes

Either Vanilla or Chocolate Frosting (see page 11) can be used to top these cupcakes, with bits of marshmallow to give texture. Crumbling cookies on top is also a good addition.

1 cup flour

a scant ¾ cup sugar

1½ teaspoons baking powder

a pinch of salt

3 tablespoons unsalted butter, at room temperature

½ cup whole milk

1 egg

¼ teaspoon pure vanilla extract

12 medium pink marshmallows

6½ oz. mini marshmallows, for the frosting

1 quantity Vanilla Frosting (page 11)

colored sanding sugar, to decorate

a 12-hole cupcake pan, lined with paper cases

Makes 12

Preheat the oven to 325°F.

Put the flour, sugar, baking powder, salt, and butter in a freestanding electric mixer with a paddle attachment (or use a handheld electric whisk) and beat on slow speed until you get a sandy consistency and everything is combined. Gradually pour in half the milk and beat until the milk is just incorporated.

Whisk the egg, vanilla, and remaining milk together in a separate bowl for a few seconds, then pour into the flour mixture and continue beating until just incorporated (scrape any unmixed ingredients from the side of the bowl with a rubber spatula). Continue mixing for a couple more minutes until the batter is smooth. Do not overmix.

Spoon the batter into the paper cases until two-thirds full and bake in the preheated oven for 20–25 minutes, or until light golden and the cake bounces back when touched. A skewer inserted in the center should come out clean. Let the cupcakes cool slightly in the pan before turning out onto a wire rack to cool completely.

Put the medium marshmallows in a heatproof bowl over a pan of simmering water. Leave until melted and smooth. When the cupcakes are cold, hollow out a small section in the center of each one and fill with a dollop of melted marshmallow. Let cool.

Stir the mini marshmallows into the Vanilla Frosting by hand until evenly dispersed.

Spoon the frosting on top of the cupcakes and decorate with sanding sugar.

ginger cupcakes

These spicy cupcakes, moistened with ginger syrup, are perfect in winter.

1 cup all-purpose flour

a scant ¾ cup sugar

1½ teaspoons baking powder

½ teaspoon ground cinnamon

¼ teaspoon ground allspice

a pinch of salt

3 tablespoons unsalted butter,
at room temperature

½ cup whole milk

1 egg

¼ teaspoon pure vanilla extract

6½ oz. stem ginger in syrup,
finely chopped (and syrup reserved),
plus extra to decorate

ginger frosting

⅓ cup whole milk

1 large piece of fresh ginger,
peeled and chopped into 4 chunks

3¼ cups confectioners' sugar, sifted

1 stick unsalted butter,
at room temperature

grated zest of ½ unwaxed lemon,
plus extra to decorate

*a 12-hole cupcake pan,
lined with paper cases*

Makes 12

For the ginger frosting, put the milk and ginger in a glass, cover, and refrigerate for a few hours, or overnight if possible.

Preheat the oven to 325°F.

Put the flour, sugar, baking powder, cinnamon, allspice, salt, and butter in a freestanding electric mixer with a paddle attachment (or use a handheld electric whisk) and beat on slow speed until you get a sandy consistency and everything is combined. Gradually pour in half the milk and beat until just incorporated. Whisk the egg, vanilla, and remaining milk together in a separate bowl for a few seconds, then pour into the flour mixture and continue beating until just incorporated (scrape any unmixed ingredients from the side of the bowl with a rubber spatula). Continue mixing for a couple more minutes until the batter is smooth. Fold in the chopped ginger.

Spoon the batter into the paper cases until two-thirds full and bake in the preheated oven for 20–25 minutes, or until golden brown and the cake bounces back when touched. While the cupcakes are baking, pour ⅓ cup of the reserved ginger syrup and ⅓ cup water into a small saucepan and bring to a boil. Boil until reduced by one-third. When the hot cupcakes come out of the oven, pour a small amount of syrup over each one. Let the cupcakes cool slightly in the pan before turning out onto a wire rack to cool completely.

For the ginger frosting: Beat together the confectioners' sugar, butter, and lemon zest in a freestanding electric mixer with a paddle attachment (or use a handheld electric whisk) on medium-slow speed until the mixture comes together and is well mixed. Turn the mixer down to slow speed. Strain the ginger-infused milk and slowly pour into the butter mixture. Once all the milk has been incorporated, turn the mixer up to high speed. Continue beating until the frosting is light and fluffy, at least 5 minutes.

When the cupcakes are cold, spoon the ginger frosting on top and finish with chopped stem ginger and lemon zest.

cakes

hummingbird cake

This cake is slightly similar to our carrot cake—moist and packed with flavor—but contains bananas and pineapple instead of carrots. The traditional recipe calls for pecans, but walnuts could also be used.

1½ cups sugar

3 eggs

1¼ cups sunflower oil

1¼ cups mashed banana

1 teaspoon ground cinnamon, plus extra to decorate

2⅓ cups all-purpose flour

1 teaspoon baking soda

½ teaspoon salt

¼ teaspoon pure vanilla extract

½ cup chopped canned pineapple

⅔ cup shelled pecans (or walnuts), chopped, plus extra, chopped and whole, to decorate

2 quantities Cream Cheese Frosting (page 11)

three 8-inch cake pans, baselined with parchment paper

Makes 10–12 slices

Preheat the oven to 325°F.

Put the sugar, eggs, oil, banana, and cinnamon in a freestanding electric mixer with a paddle attachment (or use a handheld electric whisk) and beat until all the ingredients are well incorporated (don't worry if the mixture looks slightly split). Slowly add the flour, baking soda, salt, and vanilla and continue to beat until everything is well mixed.

Stir in the chopped pineapple and pecans by hand until evenly dispersed.

Pour the batter into the prepared cake pans and smooth over with a palette knife. Bake in the preheated oven for 20–25 minutes, or until golden brown and the cake bounces back when touched. Let the cake layers cool slightly in the pans before turning out onto a wire rack to cool completely.

When the cake layers are cold, put one on a cake stand and spread about one-quarter of the Cream Cheese Frosting over it with a palette knife. Place a second layer on top and spread another quarter of the frosting over it. Top with the last layer and spread the remaining frosting over the top and sides. Finish with pecans and a light sprinkling of cinnamon.

carrot cake

Another bestseller at the Hummingbird, this carrot cake is moist and full of flavor. You can vary how finely you chop the nuts for the cake, and pecans or walnuts can be substituted freely. For an extra-special touch, decorate the top with mini carrots— these can either be formed by hand using marzipan or piped on using orange buttercream frosting.

1½ cups packed light brown sugar

3 eggs

1¼ cups sunflower oil

2⅓ cups all-purpose flour

1 teaspoon baking soda

1 teaspoon baking powder

1 teaspoon ground cinnamon, plus extra to decorate

½ teaspoon ground ginger

½ teaspoon salt

¼ teaspoon pure vanilla extract

10 oz. (about 3) carrots, grated

⅔ shelled walnuts, chopped, plus extra, chopped and whole, to decorate

2 quantities Cream Cheese Frosting (page 11)

three 8-inch cake pans, baselined with parchment paper

Makes 10–12 slices

Preheat the oven to 325°F.

Put the sugar, eggs, and oil in a freestanding electric mixer with a paddle attachment (or use a handheld electric whisk) and beat until all the ingredients are well incorporated (don't worry if the mixture looks slightly split). Slowly add the flour, baking soda, baking powder, cinnamon, ginger, salt, and vanilla and continue to beat until well mixed.

Stir in the grated carrots and walnuts by hand until they are all evenly dispersed.

Pour the batter into the prepared cake pans and smooth over with a palette knife. Bake in the preheated oven for 20–25 minutes, or until golden brown and the cake bounces back when touched. Let the cake layers cool slightly in the pans before turning out onto a wire rack to cool completely.

When the cake layers are cold, put one on a cake stand and spread about one-quarter of the Cream Cheese Frosting over it with a palette knife. Place a second layer on top and spread another quarter of the frosting over it. Top with the last layer and spread the remaining frosting over the top and sides. Finish with walnuts and a light sprinkling of cinnamon.

coconut meringue cake

This is the ultimate coconut cake. Use fresh coconut for the best results. No yolks are used in the sponge, making it airy and light. The boiled, soft meringue frosting is as light as the cake, and sprinkling grated coconut all over the top and sides of the cake makes it look extra special.

1 fresh coconut

2 cups plus 2 tablespoons sugar

1 stick unsalted butter,
at room temperature

4 cups all-purpose flour

1 tablespoon baking powder

1 cup whole milk

1 teaspoon pure vanilla extract

3 egg whites

meringue frosting

6 large egg whites

1½ cups sugar

¼ teaspoon pure vanilla extract

*three 8-inch cake pans,
baselined with parchment paper*

Makes 10–12 slices

Preheat the oven to 325°F.

Pierce the eyes of the coconut and strain the milk into a measuring cup. Add water to make 1 cup and pour into a saucepan. Add ¼ cup of the sugar and bring to a boil, stirring frequently. Set aside to cool. Heat the drained coconut in the preheated oven for about 15 minutes. Crack open the coconut and scoop out the fruit from the shell. Trim off the brown skin with a sharp knife. Grate the coconut and set aside.

Put the butter and remaining sugar in a freestanding electric mixer with a paddle attachment (or use a handheld electric whisk) and cream until light and fluffy. In a separate bowl, mix the flour and baking powder. In another bowl, mix the milk and vanilla. Beat the flour mixture into the creamed butter alternately with the milk mixture (scrape any unmixed ingredients from the side of the bowl with a rubber spatula). Beat until well mixed. In yet another bowl, whisk the egg whites with a handheld electric whisk until stiff peaks form. Using a rubber spatula, gently fold the egg whites into the cake batter until well mixed but do not overmix. Pour into the prepared cake pans and smooth with a palette knife. Bake in the preheated oven for 25–30 minutes. Let cool slightly in the pans before turning out onto a wire rack to cool.

For the meringue frosting: Put the egg whites, sugar, and ⅓ cup water in a heatproof bowl over a saucepan of simmering water. Beat slowly with an electric handheld whisk until stiff peaks form, about 7 minutes. Remove from the heat and beat in the vanilla. The frosting should be thick and glossy.

When the cake layers are cold, put one on a serving plate and drizzle with coconut syrup. Spread one-fifth of the frosting over it with a palette knife and top with grated coconut. Repeat for the next layer, then top with the third and spread the remaining frosting over the top and sides. Cover with grated coconut.

brooklyn blackout cake

This is a must for chocolate lovers. The filling and frosting are made from an eggless chocolate custard. When you make the custard, if you spread it out in a baking dish and cover it with plastic wrap, it will cool down more quickly. The cake looks amazing when covered with chocolate cake crumbs, with the almost black custard peeking through. You can refrigerate the cake to set slightly before serving.

6½ tablespoons unsalted butter, at room temperature

1¼ cups sugar

2 eggs

¼ teaspoon pure vanilla extract

⅓ cup unsweetened cocoa powder

¾ teaspoon baking powder

¾ teaspoon baking soda

a pinch of salt

1⅓ cups all-purpose flour

⅔ cup whole milk

chocolate custard

2½ cups sugar

1 tablespoon light corn syrup

1 cup unsweetened cocoa powder

1½ cups cornstarch

5½ tablespoons unsalted butter, cubed

½ teaspoon pure vanilla extract

three 8-inch cake pans, baselined with parchment paper

Makes 10–12 slices

Preheat the oven to 325°F.

Put the butter and sugar in a freestanding electric mixer with a paddle attachment (or use a handheld electric whisk) and cream until light and fluffy. Add the eggs one at a time, mixing well and scraping any unmixed ingredients from the side of the bowl with a rubber spatula after each addition. Turn the mixer down to slow speed and beat in the vanilla, cocoa, baking powder, baking soda, and salt until well mixed. Add half the flour, then all the milk, and finish with the remaining flour. Mix well until everything is well combined. Pour the batter into the prepared cake pans and smooth over with a palette knife. Bake in the preheated oven for 25–30 minutes. Let the cake layers cool slightly in the pans before turning out onto a wire rack to cool completely.

For the chocolate custard: Put the sugar, corn syrup, cocoa, and 2½ cups water into a large saucepan and bring to a boil over medium heat, whisking occasionally. Mix the cornstarch with ½–¾ cup water, whisking briskly as you add the water. The mixture should be the consistency of thick glue so add more water if it's still too thick (do not exceed 1 cup). Whisk gradually into the cocoa mixture in the pan over medium (not high) heat. Bring back to a boil, whisking constantly. Cook, whisking constantly, for a few minutes, until quite thick. Remove from the heat and stir in the butter and vanilla. Pour the custard into a bowl, cover with plastic wrap, and chill until very firm.

Slice a thin layer off one cake, put in a food processor, and process into crumbs. Put one layer on a cake stand and spread one-quarter of the chocolate custard over it. Place a second layer on top and spread another quarter of the custard over it. Top with the last layer and spread the remaining custard over the top and sides. Cover with the crumbs and chill for 2 hours.

lemon and poppy seed cake

A moist, tangy cake that is perfect with your afternoon cup of tea.

6 tablespoons unsalted butter, at room temperature

1 cup plus 1 tablespoon sugar

grated zest of 1½ unwaxed lemons

2 tablespoons poppy seeds, plus extra to decorate

⅔ cup whole milk

2 cups all-purpose flour

2 teaspoons baking powder

½ teaspoon salt

3 egg whites

lemon syrup

freshly squeezed juice and grated zest of 1 lemon

¼ cup sugar

lemon glaze

freshly squeezed juice of 1 lemon

2 cups confectioners' sugar, sifted

a 9–10-inch ring mold, greased and dusted with flour

Makes 12–16 slices

Preheat the oven to 325°F.

Put the butter, sugar, lemon zest, and poppy seeds in a freestanding electric mixer with a paddle attachment (or use a handheld electric whisk) and beat until all the ingredients are well incorporated (don't worry if the mixture looks slightly split). Slowly add the milk and continue to beat until incorporated (don't worry if the mixture looks slightly split).

In a separate bowl, combine the flour, baking powder, and salt. Add the flour mixture to the butter mixture in 3 additions, scraping any unmixed ingredients from the side of the bowl with a rubber spatula after each addition. Beat thoroughly until all the ingredients are well incorporated and the mixture is light and fluffy.

In a separate bowl, whisk the egg whites with a handheld electric whisk until stiff peaks form. Using a rubber spatula, fold the whisked egg whites into the cake batter until well mixed but do not overmix. Pour into the prepared ring mold and smooth over with a palette knife. Bake in the preheated oven for about 30 minutes, or until the cake bounces back when touched.

For the lemon syrup: While the cake is baking, put the lemon juice and zest, sugar, and ½ cup water in a small saucepan and bring to a boil over low heat. Raise the heat and boil until it has reduced by half, or until it has a thin syrup consistency. When the hot cake comes out of the oven, pour the syrup all over the top. Let cool slightly in the mold before turning out onto a wire rack to cool completely.

For the lemon glaze: Mix the lemon juice and confectioners' sugar in a bowl until smooth. It should be thick but pourable—add a little water or more sugar to thin or thicken as necessary.

When the cake is cold, put it on a cake stand, pour the glaze over it, and decorate with poppy seeds.

blueberry cake

Blueberries work so well in cakes, as they become soft and juicy and a wonderful deep purple. This cake is moist enough to be served without the frosting if you prefer.

3 sticks unsalted butter, at room temperature

1¾ cups sugar

6 eggs

1 teaspoon pure vanilla extract

3½ cups all-purpose flour

2 tablespoons plus 2 teaspoons baking powder

1 cup sour cream

3 tablespoons whole milk

1 pint fresh blueberries, plus extra to decorate

2 quantities Cream Cheese Frosting (page 11)

confectioners' sugar, to decorate

a 10-inch ring mold, greased and dusted with flour

Makes 12–16 slices

Preheat the oven to 325°F.

Put the butter and sugar in a freestanding electric mixer with a paddle attachment (or use a handheld electric whisk) and cream until light and fluffy. Add the eggs one at a time, mixing well and scraping any unmixed ingredients from the side of the bowl with a rubber spatula after each addition. Beat in the vanilla, flour, and baking powder until well mixed. Add the sour cream and milk and mix well until everything is combined and the batter is light and fluffy.

Gently stir in the blueberries by hand until evenly dispersed.

Pour the batter into the prepared ring mold and smooth over with a palette knife. Bake in the preheated oven for 40 minutes, or until golden brown and the cake bounces back when touched. Let the cake cool slightly in the mold before turning out onto a wire rack to cool completely.

When the cake is cold, put it on a serving plate, cover the top and sides with the Cream Cheese Frosting, and decorate with more blueberries. Dust with confectioners' sugar.

coffee cake

This is not as sweet than some of the other cakes in this chapter, but you could top it with Chocolate Frosting (see page 11) to turn into a mocha cake for a sweeter tooth.

2 tablespoons instant coffee granules

3 sticks plus 6 tablespoons unsalted butter, at room temperature

2¼ cups sugar

8 eggs

3½ cups all-purpose flour

2 tablespoons baking powder

2 teaspoons unsweetened cocoa powder, plus extra to decorate

1 quantity Vanilla Frosting (page 11)

2 oz. bittersweet chocolate, grated with a cheese grater into shavings

coffee beans, to decorate (optional)

a 10-inch ring mold,
greased and dusted with flour

Makes 12–16 slices

To make a coffee essence, put the instant coffee granules and ⅔ cup water in a small saucepan and bring to a boil over medium heat. Boil until reduced by half, then remove from the heat and let cool completely. Set aside a tablespoon of the essence to use in the frosting.

Preheat the oven to 325°F.

Put the butter, sugar, and cold coffee essence in a freestanding electric mixer with a paddle attachment (or use a handheld electric whisk) and beat until all the ingredients are well incorporated. Add the eggs one at a time, mixing well and scraping any unmixed ingredients from the side of the bowl with a rubber spatula after each addition. Beat in the flour, baking powder, and cocoa and mix well until everything is combined and the batter is light and fluffy.

Pour the batter into the prepared ring mold and smooth over with a palette knife. Bake in the preheated oven for 40 minutes, or until the cake feels firm to the touch. (Do not open the oven while the cake is baking, as it will sink.) Let the cake cool slightly in the mold before turning out onto a wire rack to cool completely.

Stir the reserved tablespoon of coffee essence into the Vanilla Frosting until evenly mixed.

When the cake is cold, put it on a serving plate, cover the top with the frosting, and dust with a light sprinkling of cocoa. Decorate with the chocolate shavings and coffee beans, if using.

spiced pound cake

This is more flavorful than a regular pound cake, with lots of spices to liven it up. It's another not-too-sweet cake that's perfect with a cup of tea or coffee.

2 sticks unsalted butter,
at room temperature

3¼ cups sugar

5 eggs

1 cup whole milk

1 teaspoon pure vanilla extract

¼ teaspoon lemon extract

¼ teaspoon ground cloves

¼ teaspoon ground cinnamon

¼ teaspoon ground ginger

¼ teaspoon ground nutmeg

3 cups plus 2 tablespoons
all-purpose flour

½ teaspoon baking soda

½ teaspoon salt

*a 10-inch ring mold,
greased and dusted with flour*

Makes 12–16 slices

Preheat the oven to 325°F.

Put the butter and sugar in a freestanding electric mixer with a paddle attachment (or use a handheld electric whisk) and cream until light and fluffy. Add the eggs one at a time, mixing well and scraping any unmixed ingredients from the side of the bowl with a rubber spatula after each addition. Beat in the milk, vanilla, and lemon extract until well mixed.

Sift the cloves, cinnamon, ginger, nutmeg, flour, baking soda, and salt into a separate bowl, then add to the butter mixture and beat until all the ingredients are well combined.

Pour the batter into the prepared ring mold and smooth over with a palette knife. Bake in the preheated oven for 60–70 minutes, or until golden brown and a skewer inserted in the cake comes out clean. Let cool slightly in the mold before turning out onto a wire rack to cool completely.

buttermilk pound loaf

Here's a reliable, traditional pound cake recipe—moist with butter and not too sweet. You can add chocolate chips, nuts, or berries to the cake batter as an alternative.

1 stick unsalted butter, at room temperature

1⅔ cups sugar

3 eggs

1½ cups all-purpose flour

½ teaspoon baking soda

½ teaspoon salt

½ cup buttermilk

¼ teaspoon pure vanilla extract

a 9 x 5-inch loaf pan, greased and dusted with flour

Makes 8–10 slices

Preheat the oven to 325°F.

Put the butter and sugar in a freestanding electric mixer with a paddle attachment (or use a handheld electric whisk) and cream until light and fluffy. Add the eggs one at a time, mixing well and scraping any unmixed ingredients from the side of the bowl with a rubber spatula after each addition.

Sift the flour, baking soda, and salt into a separate bowl. Add one-third of the flour mixture to the butter mixture, followed by half the buttermilk. Mix well. Repeat this process, then finish with the remaining flour mixture. Stir in the vanilla. Mix well until all the ingredients are well combined.

Pour the batter into the prepared loaf pan and smooth over with a palette knife. Bake in the preheated oven for 35–40 minutes, or until golden brown and the cake bounces back when touched. Let the cake cool slightly in the pan before turning out onto a wire rack to cool completely.

banana bread

We go through several of these loaves every day at the Hummingbird. Try to use very ripe bananas for a sweeter, richer cake.

1⅛ cups packed light brown sugar

2 eggs

1 scant cup mashed banana

2¼ cups all-purpose flour

1 teaspoon baking powder

1 teaspoon baking soda

1 teaspoon ground cinnamon

1 teaspoon ground ginger

1 stick plus 2 tablespoons unsalted butter, melted

*a 9 x 5-inch loaf pan,
greased and dusted with flour*

Makes 8–10 slices

Preheat the oven to 325°F.

Put the sugar and eggs in a freestanding electric mixer with a paddle attachment (or use a handheld electric whisk) and beat until well incorporated. Beat in the mashed banana.

Add the flour, baking powder, baking soda, cinnamon, and ginger to the sugar mixture. Mix it thoroughly until all the dry ingredients have been incorporated into the egg mixture. Pour in the melted butter and beat until all the ingredients are well mixed.

Pour the batter into the prepared loaf pan and smooth over with a palette knife. Bake in the preheated oven for about 1 hour, or until firm to the touch and a skewer inserted in the center comes out clean. Let the cake cool slightly in the pan before turning out onto a wire rack to cool completely.

nutty apple loaf

This cake is very popular in the winter months. We use chopped mixed nuts, but you could use your own combination of favorite nuts. The chunks of cooked apple in the cake give it a wonderful texture and flavor.

1½ sticks unsalted butter, at room temperature

¾ cup packed light brown sugar

2 tablespoons strawberry jam

2 eggs

1 cup plus 2 tablespoons all-purpose flour

1 tablespoon baking powder

1 teaspoon ground cinnamon

⅓ cup shelled mixed nuts, chopped

1½ oz. bittersweet chocolate, roughly chopped

2 eating apples, peeled, cored, and roughly chopped

a 9 x 5-inch loaf pan, greased and dusted with flour

Makes 8–10 slices

Put the butter, sugar, and strawberry jam in a freestanding electric mixer with a paddle attachment (or use a handheld electric whisk) and cream until light and fluffy. Add the eggs one at a time, mixing well and scraping any unmixed ingredients from the side of the bowl with a rubber spatula after each addition.

Sift together the flour, baking powder, and cinnamon in a separate bowl, then beat into the butter mixture. Stir the nuts, chocolate, and apples into the mixture by hand until evenly dispersed. Cover and refrigerate for a few hours, or overnight if possible.

Preheat the oven to 325°F.

Pour the batter into the prepared loaf pan and smooth over with a palette knife. Bake in the preheated oven for 50–60 minutes, or until brown and the cake feels firm to the touch. A skewer inserted in the center should come out clean, but for a little melted chocolate. Let the cake cool slightly in the pan before turning out onto a wire rack to cool completely.

lemon loaf

When drizzled with the lemon syrup, this is incredibly moist and tangy and flies off our counter when served in the shop.

1½ cups plus 2 tablespoons sugar

3 eggs

grated zest of 2 unwaxed lemons

2¾ cups all-purpose flour

1½ teaspoons baking powder

1 teaspoon salt

1 cup whole milk

½ teaspoon pure vanilla extract

1 stick plus 5 tablespoons unsalted butter, melted

lemon syrup

freshly squeezed juice and grated zest of 1 lemon

¼ cup sugar

a 9 x 5-inch loaf pan, greased and dusted with flour

Makes 8–10 slices

Preheat the oven to 325°F.

Put the sugar, eggs, and lemon zest in a freestanding electric mixer with a paddle attachment (or use a handheld electric whisk) and beat until well mixed.

Sift the flour, baking powder, and salt into a separate bowl. Combine the milk and vanilla in another bowl. Add one-third of the flour mixture to the sugar mixture and beat well, then beat in one-third of the milk mixture. Repeat this process twice more until everything has been added. Turn the mixer up to high speed and beat until the mixture is light and fluffy.

Turn the mixer down to low speed, pour in the melted butter, and beat until well incorporated.

Pour the batter into the prepared loaf pan and bake in the preheated oven for about 1 hour 15 minutes, or until golden brown and the loaf bounces back when touched.

For the lemon syrup: While the cake is baking, put the lemon juice and zest, sugar, and ¹/₂ cup water in a small saucepan and bring to a boil over low heat. Raise the heat and boil until it has reduced by half, or until it has a thin syrup consistency. When the hot cake comes out of the oven, put it on a wire rack in the sink and pour the syrup over the top. The excess syrup will run over the edges into the sink. Let cool slightly in the pan before turning out onto a wire rack to cool completely.

new york cheesecake

A plain baked New York cheesecake is always extremely popular. It's important not to overbeat the ingredients—stop mixing as soon as each ingredient you add is just incorporated. You may think the cake isn't fully baked when you take it out of the oven, but it will set into a perfect cheesecake overnight! You can also fold in chopped cookies, brownies, or berries just before baking to make a flavored cheesecake.

1 lb. 14 oz. cream cheese

1 scant cup sugar

1 teaspoon pure vanilla extract

4 eggs

crust

1 cup plus 2 tablespoons
all-purpose flour

¼ teaspoon baking powder

¼ cup sugar

3½ tablespoons unsalted butter

1 egg yolk

*a 9-inch springform cake pan, greased
and baselined with parchment paper*

Makes 10–12 slices

Preheat the oven to 300°F.

For the crust: Put the flour, baking powder, sugar, and butter in a freestanding electric mixer with a paddle attachment (or use a handheld electric whisk) and beat until you get a sandy consistency.

Add the egg yolk and mix through—it will still be sandy but it will be a little more moist. Press this mixture into the base of the prepared cake pan, using the ball of your hand or a tablespoon to flatten and compress it. It must be pressed down to form a dense base.

Bake in the preheated oven for 20–25 minutes, or until golden brown. It should have lost its sandy texture and come together to form a coherent base. Set aside to cool.

Put the cream cheese, sugar, and vanilla in a freestanding electric mixer with a paddle attachment (or use a handheld electric whisk) and beat on slow speed until you get a very smooth, thick mixture. Add one egg at a time, while still mixing. Scrape any unmixed ingredients from the side of the bowl with a rubber spatula after adding the second and last eggs. The mixture should be very smooth and creamy. The mixer can be turned up to a higher speed at the end to make the mix a little lighter and fluffier, but be careful not to overmix otherwise the cheese will split.

Spoon the mixture onto the cold cheesecake crust. Put the pan inside a larger pan or in a deep baking dish and fill with water until it reaches two-thirds of the way up the cake pan. Bake for 30–40 minutes, or until golden brown but still wobbly in the center. Don't overcook. Let the cheesecake cool slightly in the pan, then cover and refrigerate overnight before serving.

chocolate cheesecake

There must be a chocolate version of everything, so chocolate lovers don't have to miss out! Using the best-quality bittersweet chocolate in this cheesecake will make the finished result taste so much better. A mix of triple chocolate chips (bittersweet, milk, and white) can be folded in before baking for an extra chocolate kick.

1 lb. 14 oz. cream cheese

1 cup sugar

1 teaspoon pure vanilla extract

4 eggs

6½ oz. bittersweet chocolate, roughly chopped

crust

6½ oz. graham crackers

2 tablespoons unsweetened cocoa powder

1 stick plus 2 tablespoons unsalted butter, melted

a 9-inch springform cake pan, greased and baselined with parchment paper

Makes 10–12 slices

Preheat the oven to 300°F.

For the crust: Roughly break up the graham crackers and put them in a food processor with the cocoa. Process until finely ground. Slowly pour the melted butter into the processor while the motor is running. Press this mixture into the base of the prepared cake pan, using the ball of your hand or a tablespoon to flatten and compress it. Refrigerate while you make the topping.

Put the cream cheese, sugar, and vanilla in a freestanding electric mixer with a paddle attachment (or use a handheld electric whisk) and beat on slow speed until you get a very smooth, thick mixture. Add one egg at a time, while still mixing. Scrape any unmixed ingredients from the side of the bowl with a rubber spatula after adding the second and last eggs. The mixture should be very smooth and creamy. The mixer can be turned up to a higher speed at the end to make the mix a little lighter and fluffier, but be careful not to overmix otherwise the cheese will split.

Put the chocolate in a heatproof bowl over a saucepan of simmering water (do not let the base of the bowl touch the water). Leave until melted and smooth. Spoon a little of the cream cheese mixture into the melted chocolate, stir to mix, then add a little more. This will even out the temperatures of the 2 mixtures. Eventually stir all the cream cheese mixture into the chocolate mixture and mix until well combined and smooth.

Spoon the mixture onto the cold cheesecake crust. Put the pan inside a larger pan or in a deep baking dish and fill with water until it reaches two-thirds of the way up the cake pan. Bake for 40–50 minutes, checking regularly after 40 minutes to make sure it isn't burning. Don't overcook—it should be wobbly in the center. Let the cheesecake cool slightly in the pan, then cover and refrigerate overnight before serving.

icebox banana cheesecake

This is another take on a cheesecake, but it is set and has a firmer texture than baked cheesecake. This recipe contains gelatin, so vegetarians will have to use a vegetarian alternative and follow the manufacturer's instructions.

1½ envelopes (10 g) granulated gelatin

1 cup mashed banana, plus extra sliced bananas to decorate

⅓ cup orange juice

10 oz. cream cheese

½ cup sugar

3 egg yolks

1 cup heavy cream

crust

6½ oz. graham crackers

1 stick plus 2 tablespoons unsalted butter, melted

a 9-inch springform cake pan, greased and baselined with parchment paper

Makes 10–12 slices

For the crust: Roughly break up the graham crackers and put them in a food processor. Process until finely ground. Slowly pour the melted butter into the processor while the motor is running. Press this mixture into the base of the prepared cake pan, using the ball of your hand or a tablespoon to flatten and compress it. Refrigerate while you make the topping.

Pour ⅓ cup water into a small bowl. Sprinkle the gelatin into the water. Set aside for at least 5 minutes.

Put the mashed banana and orange juice in a saucepan and heat over medium heat until the bananas are cooked though. Set aside to cool slightly.

Put the cream cheese, sugar, and egg yolks in a freestanding electric mixer with a paddle attachment (or use a handheld electric whisk) and beat on slow speed until you get a very smooth, thick mixture.

In a separate bowl, using a handheld electric whisk, whip the cream until thick but not stiff. Gently fold into the cream cheese mixture by hand. Set aside.

Stir the soaked gelatin into the warm—not hot—banana and orange juice mixture. Stir well until all the gelatin is evenly dispersed. Spoon a little of the cream cheese mixture into the banana mixture and stir to mix, then add a little more. This will even out the temperatures of the 2 mixtures and prevent the gelatin from setting in lumps. Eventually stir all the banana mixture into the cream cheese mixture and mix until well combined and smooth.

Spoon the mixture onto the cold cheesecake crust and let cool completely. Cover and refrigerate for 2 hours, or overnight if possible. Decorate with slices of banana before serving.

pies

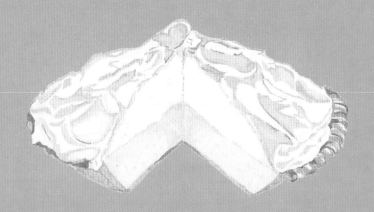

basic pie crust

This simple pie crust is used in most of the recipes in this chapter. You will either need to bake it blind and top with a pie filling that doesn't need any further baking, or if the filling needs to be cooked, then only partially blind bake the crust.

2 cups all-purpose flour

½ teaspoon salt

7½ tablespoons unsalted butter

a 9-inch pie dish, greased
baking beans

Makes enough for a single crust pie

Put the flour, salt, and butter in an electric mixer with a paddle attachment and beat on slow speed until you get a sandy consistency and everything is combined. Add 1 tablespoon water and beat until well mixed. Add a second tablespoon of water and beat until you have a smooth, even dough. If the dough is still a little dry, add another tablespoon of water, but be careful not to add too much water—it is safer to beat the dough at high speed to try to bring the ingredients together.

Wrap the dough in plastic wrap and let rest for 1 hour.

Preheat the oven to 325°F.

Lightly dust a clean work surface with flour and roll out the dough with a rolling pin. Line the prepared pie dish with the dough and trim the edges with a sharp knife. Lay a sheet of parchment paper over the dough crust and pour in the baking beans.

To blind bake (for a pie that WILL NOT need baking again):
Bake the pie crust in the preheated oven for about 15–20 minutes, or until the edges are light golden and partially cooked. Remove the parchment paper and baking beans and bake for a further 15–20 minutes. Take care not to overbake—the edges should be light golden.

To partially blind bake (for a pie that WILL need baking again):
Bake the pie crust in the preheated oven for about 10 minutes. Remove the parchment paper and baking beans and bake for a further 10 minutes. The dough should still be pale and slightly raw in the center.

lemon meringue pie

This old favorite never lasts long when we put it out on our shelves! The meringue topping should be generous and tall. There are two options for making the meringue in the recipe below: the Italian is our authentic version, but the nervous baker can use the simpler version. Use a warm knife when cutting the pie—it keeps the slices neat. The sliced pie looks amazing with the bright yellow filling and white, fluffy topping.

8 egg yolks

2 x 13.5-oz. cans condensed milk

freshly squeezed juice and grated zest of 8 unwaxed lemons

1 Basic Pie Crust, partially blind baked (page 80)

simpler meringue topping

6 egg whites

1¾ cups sugar

1 teaspoon pure vanilla extract

OR Italian meringue topping

2 cups sugar

7 egg whites

¼ teaspoon pure vanilla extract

Makes 10–12 slices

Preheat the oven to 300°F.

Put the egg yolks, condensed milk, and lemon juice and zest in a glass bowl and mix gently with a balloon whisk until all the ingredients are very well incorporated. The mixture will thicken naturally.

Pour into the partially blind-baked pie crust and bake in the preheated oven for 20–30 minutes. The filling should be firm to the touch but still very slightly soft in the center (not wobbly!). Let cool completely, then cover and refrigerate for at least 1 hour, or overnight if possible.

For the simpler meringue topping: Preheat the oven to 300°F.

Put the egg whites in a freestanding electric mixer with a whisk attachment and beat until frothy. Gradually add 2 tablespoons of the sugar at a time, beating well after each addition. Once you have beaten in all the sugar, add the vanilla and beat again until stiff peaks form.

Spoon the meringue on top of the cold pie, making sure you completely cover the pie filling. Create peaks and swirls in the top of the meringue with the back of a tablespoon.

Bake in the preheated oven for about 20 minutes, or until the meringue is golden brown and crisp to the touch. (With this method, the egg whites are not cooked through, so please see the note on page 4 about uncooked or partially cooked eggs.) Let cool completely before serving.

For the Italian meringue topping: Preheat the oven to 300°F.

Put the sugar in a small saucepan and just cover with water. Set over medium heat and bring to a boil.

While the sugar is on the stovetop, put the egg whites in a freestanding electric mixer with a whisk attachment (or use a handheld electric whisk) on medium-slow speed. Beat until the egg whites are light and foamy. When the sugar has been boiling for a short while, it should reach soft ball stage (see below).

Turn the mixer up to medium-high speed and slowly pour the sugar syrup into the egg whites. Once all the syrup is incorporated, turn the mixer up to maximum speed and beat for about 10–15 minutes, or until the meringue has tripled in size and is very white and fluffy. Turn the mixer back down to medium speed and continue to beat for a couple more minutes until the meringue has cooled down slightly.

Spoon the meringue on top of the cold pie, making sure you completely cover the pie filling. Create peaks and swirls in the top of the meringue with the back of a tablespoon.

Bake in the preheated oven for about 20 minutes, or until the meringue is golden brown and crisp to the touch. Let cool completely before serving.

Soft ball stage: When the sugar has been boiling for a short while, the appearance of the bubbles starts to change from very watery to more syrupy. Dip a spoon into the sugar, then drop it directly into a glass of cold water. The sugar will firm up on contact with the water. You should be able to form a soft ball out of the sugar, in which case it has reached soft ball stage. If it sets too hard to be able to form a ball, it has been boiled too long and has reached hard ball stage. Be careful, as the sugar goes from soft ball stage to hard ball stage very quickly. Don't touch the hot syrup with your bare hands until you have dipped the spoon into the glass of cold water, otherwise you will burn your fingers!

pecan pie

Sweet and sticky, this is a quintessentially American dessert that the Brits visiting The Hummingbird Bakery are growing to love too. It's one of the pies that I knew I wanted to sell as soon as I thought of opening the Bakery.

1 quantity Basic Pie Crust dough, unbaked (page 80)

1 cup sugar

1 cup dark corn syrup

½ teaspoon salt

3 eggs

4 tablespoons unsalted butter, cubed

¼ teaspoon pure vanilla extract

⅔ cup shelled pecans, chopped, plus extra pecan halves to decorate

a 9-inch pie dish, greased

Makes 10–12 slices

Preheat the oven to 325°F.

Lightly dust a clean work surface with flour and roll out the dough with a rolling pin. Line the prepared pie dish with the dough and trim the edges with a sharp knife.

Put the sugar, corn syrup, and salt in a large saucepan over medium heat. Bring to a boil, then remove from the heat and let cool slightly.

In a separate bowl, whisk the eggs briefly with a balloon whisk until they are just mixed. Slowly pour the warm (not hot) syrup into the eggs, stirring briskly so that you don't allow the eggs time to scramble.

Add the butter and vanilla to the bowl and stir until the butter has melted and is evenly dispersed.

Put the chopped pecans into the pie crust, then pour the filling on top. Arrange the pecan halves gently on top of the filling around the edge of the pie. Bake in the preheated oven for about 50–60 minutes, or until a dark, caramel color with a slightly crusty surface.

key lime pie

We don't use any food coloring in our lime filling, just a bit of lime zest. Our Key Lime Pie is topped with a mound of freshly whipped cream, but you can use the same meringue as the Lemon Meringue Pie (see pages 81–82).

8 egg yolks

2 x 13.5-oz. cans condensed milk

freshly squeezed juice and grated zest of 5 limes, plus extra grated zest to decorate

2 cups whipping cream

crust

1 lb. graham crackers

1 stick plus 6 tablespoons unsalted butter, melted

a 9-inch pie dish, greased

Makes 10–12 slices

Preheat the oven to 325°F.

For the crust: Roughly break up the graham crackers and put them in a food processor. Process until finely ground. Slowly pour the melted butter into the processor while the motor is running. Press this mixture into the base and neatly up the side of the prepared pie dish, using the ball of your hand or a tablespoon to flatten and compress it.

Bake in the preheated oven for about 20 minutes, or until deep golden and firm. Set aside to cool completely.

Turn the oven down to 300°F.

Put the egg yolks, condensed milk, and lime juice and zest in a glass bowl and mix gently with a balloon whisk until all the ingredients are very well incorporated. The mixture will thicken naturally.

Pour into the cold pie crust and bake in the preheated oven for 20–30 minutes. The filling should be firm to the touch but still very slightly soft in the center (not wobbly!). Let cool completely, then cover and refrigerate for at least 1 hour, or overnight if possible.

When you are ready to serve the pie, whip the cream with a handheld electric whisk in a large bowl until soft peaks form, then spread over the pie and decorate with a little lime zest.

pumpkin pie

The classic Thanksgiving pie, Pumpkin Pie is incredibly easy to make. The finished pie looks rustic and simple, with a deep golden-orange filling. If you don't want to leave it plain, you can cover it in whipped cream, but plain is more traditional.

1 quantity Basic Pie Crust dough, unbaked (page 80)

1 egg

14-oz. can pumpkin purée

8-oz. can evaporated milk

1 cup plus 2 tablespoons sugar

¼ teaspoon ground cloves

1 teaspoon salt

¾ teaspoon ground cinnamon, plus extra to decorate

¼ teaspoon ground ginger

1 tablespoon all-purpose flour

lightly whipped cream, to serve (optional)

a 9-inch pie dish, greased

Makes 10–12 slices

Preheat the oven to 325°F.

Lightly dust a clean work surface with flour and roll out the dough with a rolling pin. Line the prepared pie dish with the dough and trim the edges with a sharp knife.

Put the egg, pumpkin purée, evaporated milk, sugar, cloves, salt, cinnamon, ginger, and flour in a large bowl and mix with a wooden spoon until everything is well combined and there are no lumps.

Pour into the pie crust and bake in the preheated oven for about 30–40 minutes, or until the filling is set firm and doesn't wobble when shaken.

Let cool completely, then serve with a dollop of lightly whipped cream, if using, and a light sprinkling of cinnamon.

mississippi mud pie

Our version of Mississippi Mud Pie has a rich, cooked chocolate pudding filling, topped with a mountain of whipped cream. You can finish the pie with grated chocolate or cocoa powder. This is another pie that is extremely popular and sells out fast.

5 oz. bittersweet chocolate, roughly chopped, plus extra, grated with a cheese grater into shavings, to decorate

3½ tablespoons unsalted butter

2 tablespoons light corn syrup

6 eggs

1½ cups packed light brown sugar

1 teaspoon pure vanilla extract

1 Basic Pie Crust, partially blind baked (page 80)

1½ cups whipping cream

Makes 10–12 slices

Preheat the oven to 325°F.

Put the chocolate, butter, and corn syrup in a heatproof bowl over a saucepan of simmering water (do not let the base of the bowl touch the water). Leave until melted and smooth, then remove from the heat and let cool slightly.

While the chocolate mixture is melting, put the eggs, sugar, and vanilla in a freestanding electric mixer with a paddle attachment (or use a handheld electric whisk) and beat until well combined.

Gradually beat the warm chocolate mixture into the egg mixture on slow speed. Make sure the chocolate isn't too hot, otherwise it will scramble the eggs. Beat thoroughly until smooth.

Pour into the partially blind-baked pie crust and bake in the preheated oven for about 35–40 minutes. Check regularly after 30 minutes to make sure it isn't burning. The baked pie should be firm to the touch but still have a slight wobble in the center. Let cool completely, then cover and refrigerate overnight.

When you are ready to serve the pie, whip the cream with a handheld electric whisk in a large bowl until soft peaks form, then spread over the pie and finish with chocolate shavings.

banana cream pie

For this pie, you blind bake the pastry but the filling itself is not baked—the pie is simply filled with a custard full of banana chunks. As with all banana recipes, it's best to use very ripe bananas. Be generous with the whipped cream topping, and dust liberally with cinnamon. The base is covered with dulce de leche—a delicious South American soft caramel that is now easily found in supermarkets.

7 tablespoons dulce de leche

1 Basic Pie Crust, fully blind baked (page 80)

3 large bananas, peeled and sliced, plus extra to decorate

1¾ cups whipping cream

ground cinnamon, to decorate

custard

2¼ cups whole milk

¼ teaspoon pure vanilla extract

5 egg yolks

1 cup sugar

⅓ cup all-purpose flour

⅓ cup cornstarch

Makes 10–12 slices

Preheat the oven to 325°F.

For the custard: Put 1⅔ cups of the milk and the vanilla in a medium saucepan over medium heat and bring to a boil. Remove from the heat and let cool down very slightly.

Put the egg yolks, sugar, flour, cornstarch, and remaining milk in a separate bowl and mix well to form a smooth paste.

Pour a little of the hot milk mixture into the egg mixture and stir well to combine. Pour the remaining milk mixture into the egg mixture and stir well until all the ingredients are combined.

Pour everything back into the saucepan over low heat and bring to a boil, whisking continuously with a balloon whisk. Cook until thick, about 5 minutes. Pour the custard into a bowl, lay plastic wrap directly on top (to stop a skin forming), and let cool completely.

Spread the dulce de leche over the base of the pie crust and arrange the slices of banana over it. Spoon the cold custard over the top. Cover and refrigerate for a couple of hours until the custard has set completely.

When you are ready to serve the pie, whip the cream with a handheld electric whisk in a large bowl until soft peaks form, then spread over the pie and decorate with more slices of banana. Finish with a generous sprinkling of cinnamon.

apple pie

You can't go wrong with a slice of warm, classic apple pie served with a scoop of vanilla ice cream! For more skilled home-bakers, it's fun to decorate the top layer of pastry with cut-out leaves and other shapes. Be sure to brush the top with an egg wash and sprinkle with sugar to get a beautiful golden finish. Do also use firm, tart apples such as Granny Smiths, as they hold their shape and prevent the filling from becoming too sweet.

2 quantities Basic Pie Crust dough, unbaked (page 80)

1 stick plus 2 tablespoons unsalted butter

3 teaspoons ground cinnamon

3½ lbs. green apples, peeled, cored, and cut into medium slices

1 cup sugar, plus extra to sprinkle

1 egg, mixed with a little milk

a 9-inch pie dish, greased

Makes 10–12 slices

Preheat the oven to 325°F.

Lightly dust a clean work surface with flour. Divide the dough in half. Roll out one half with a rolling pin, use to line the prepared pie dish, and trim the edges with a sharp knife.

Put the butter and cinnamon in a large saucepan and heat until the butter has melted. Add the apples and stir until they are well coated in butter. Finally, add the sugar and stir again. Cook the apples until softened but not cooked through, then spread them out in a shallow dish to cool completely.

Fill the pie crust with the cold apples. Lightly dust a clean work surface with flour again. Roll out the remaining half of the dough with a rolling pin, drape over the pie dish, and press down the edges, pinching to make a textured edge. Trim any excess with a sharp knife.

Make 3 slits in the lid of the pie to let the steam out while the pie is cooking. Make leaf shapes out of the pastry trimmings and use to decorate the pie. Brush the egg-and-milk wash over the top of the pie with a pastry brush and sprinkle with a little extra sugar. Bake in the preheated oven for about 30–40 minutes, or until the pastry is golden brown. Let cool completely before serving.

blueberry pie

This is a summer favorite that should be made with lots of fresh, ripe blueberries. The cornstarch thickens the filling as it cooks and keeps it firm enough to allow the pie to be sliced. The filling should bubble through the cuts made in the pastry lid, which is when you know the pie is ready.

2 quantities Basic Pie Crust dough, unbaked (page 80)

½ cup sugar

3 tablespoons cornstarch

2 tablespoons freshly squeezed lemon juice

2 teaspoons grated lemon zest

2 pints blueberries

a 9-inch pie dish, greased

Makes 10–12 slices

Lightly dust a clean work surface with flour. Divide the dough in half. Roll out one half with a rolling pin, use to line the prepared pie dish, and trim the edges with a sharp knife.

Put the sugar, cornstarch, lemon juice and zest, and blueberries in a bowl and mix well. Fill the pie crust with the blueberry mixture. Lightly dust a clean work surface with flour again. Roll out the remaining half of the dough with a rolling pin, drape over the pie dish, and press down the edges, pinching to make a textured edge. Trim any excess with a sharp knife.

Make 3 slits in the lid of the pie to let the steam out while the pie is cooking. Let the pie rest in the refrigerator for 1 hour before baking.

Preheat the oven to 325°F.

Bake the pie in the preheated oven for about 40–50 minutes, or until the filling is bubbling thickly. After 30 minutes of baking, protect the edges from overcooking by covering them with foil. Let cool completely before serving.

brownies and bars

traditional brownies

Traditional brownies must be chewy, chocolatey, and dense. Many other brownie recipes seen outside the USA are not really brownies! We don't put nuts in this traditional recipe, but you can add walnuts or pecans if you like. These brownies are so popular in London, we sell several trays every day. For chocolate overload, you can put chocolate chips into the mixture before baking!

6½ oz. bittersweet chocolate, roughly chopped

1½ sticks unsalted butter

1⅔ cups sugar

1 cup all-purpose flour

3 eggs

confectioners' sugar, to decorate

a 13 x 9-inch baking pan, lined with parchment paper

Makes about 12–15 portions

Preheat the oven to 325°F.

Put the chocolate and butter in a heatproof bowl over a saucepan of simmering water (do not let the base of the bowl touch the water). Leave until melted and smooth.

Remove from the heat. Add the sugar and stir until well incorporated. Add the flour and stir until well incorporated. Finally, stir in the eggs and mix until thick and smooth.

Spoon the dough into the prepared baking pan and bake in the preheated oven for about 30–35 minutes, or until flaky on the top but still soft in the center. Be careful not to overbake otherwise the edges will become hard and crunchy. Let cool completely before dusting with confectioners' sugar, to decorate.

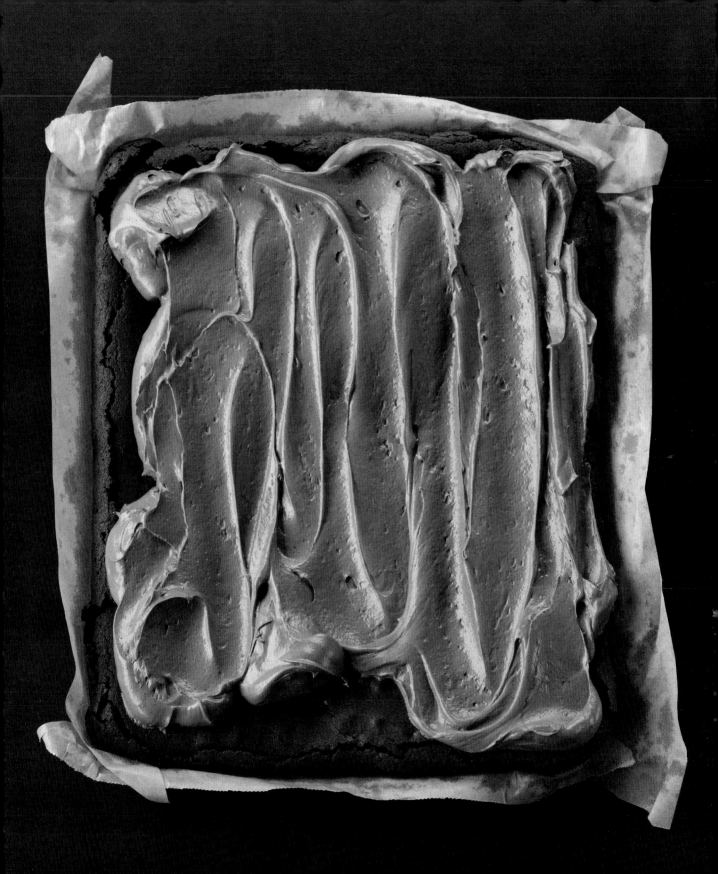

frosted brownies

Our alternative to the traditional brownie, this version is more cake-like, contains nuts, and is topped with chocolatey cream-cheese frosting.

5 eggs

2½ cups sugar

1 cup all-purpose flour

¾ cup plus 2 tablespoons unsweetened cocoa powder

2 sticks unsalted butter, melted

¼ cup shelled walnuts, chopped

2 oz. bittersweet chocolate, roughly chopped

frosting

1½ cups confectioners' sugar, sifted

5 tablespoons unsalted butter, at room temperature

¼ cup unsweetened cocoa powder, sifted

5 oz. cream cheese, cold

a 13 x 9-inch baking pan lined with parchment paper

Makes about 12–15 portions

Preheat the oven to 325°F.

Put the eggs and sugar in a large bowl and beat with a handheld electric whisk until light and fluffy. Add the flour and cocoa and beat until all the ingredients are well mixed. Pour in the melted butter and mix through. Stir the walnuts and chocolate in by hand until evenly dispersed.

Spoon the mixture into the prepared baking pan and bake in the preheated oven for about 30–35 minutes, or until the top is firm but the center is still soft. Let cool completely.

For the frosting: Beat together the confectioners' sugar, butter, and cocoa in a freestanding electric mixer with a paddle attachment (or use a handheld electric whisk) on medium-slow speed until the mixture comes together and is well mixed. Add the cream cheese in one go and beat until it is completely incorporated. Turn the mixer up to medium-high speed. Continue beating until the frosting is light and fluffy, at least 5 minutes. Do not overbeat, as it can quickly become runny.

When the brownies are cold, spread the frosting over the top.

raspberry cheesecake brownies

This triple-layer dessert looks irresistible when sliced: a slim layer of brownie topped with cheesecake and covered with raspberry-flavored whipped cream. The three elements combine beautifully. You can substitute other berries in season if you like.

brownie dough

6½ oz. bittersweet chocolate, roughly chopped

1 stick plus 5 tablespoons unsalted butter

2 cups confectioners' sugar

3 eggs

1 scant cup all-purpose flour

cheesecake

14 oz. cream cheese

1¼ cups confectioners' sugar

½ teaspoon pure vanilla extract

2 eggs

cream topping

1¼ cups whipping cream

¾ cup confectioners' sugar

1 cup raspberries, plus extra to decorate

a 13 x 9-inch baking pan, lined with parchment paper

Makes about 12–15 portions

Preheat the oven to 170°C (325°F) Gas 3.

For the brownie dough: Put the chocolate in a heatproof bowl over a pan of simmering water (do not let the base of the bowl touch the water). Leave until melted and smooth. Put the butter and sugar in a freestanding electric mixer with a paddle attachment and beat until all the ingredients are well incorporated. Add the eggs one at a time, mixing well and scraping any unmixed ingredients from the side of the bowl with a rubber spatula after each addition. Gradually beat in the flour, mixing well after each addition, then turn the mixer up to high speed and beat for a little longer until you get a smooth mixture. Slowly pour in the melted chocolate and mix thoroughly. Pour into the prepared baking pan and smooth over with a palette knife.

For the cheesecake: Put the cream cheese, sugar, and vanilla in a freestanding electric mixer with a paddle attachment and beat on slow speed until smooth and thick. Add one egg at a time, while still mixing. Scrape any unmixed ingredients from the side of the bowl with a rubber spatula after each addition. The mixture should be very smooth and creamy. The mixer can be turned up to a higher speed at the end to make the mix a little lighter and fluffier, but be careful not to overmix, otherwise the cheese will split. Spoon on top of the brownie base and smooth over with a palette knife. Bake in the preheated oven for 30–40 minutes, or until the cheesecake is firm to the touch and light golden around the edges. The center should still be pale. Let cool completely, then cover and refrigerate for 2 hours, or overnight if possible.

For the cream topping: Put the cream, sugar, and raspberries in a freestanding electric mixer with a whisk attachment and beat until firm but not stiff. Turn the brownies out onto a board and turn right-side up. Spread the topping evenly over the brownies and decorate with more raspberries.

blondies

Here's an alternative to brownies for those who don't like the rich taste of chocolate; these blondies are made with white chocolate.

5 oz. white chocolate, roughly chopped

1 stick unsalted butter

¾ cup sugar

2 eggs

1½ teaspoons pure vanilla extract

1½ cups all-purpose flour

a pinch of salt

1 scant cup shelled pecans, chopped

a 13 x 9-inch baking pan, lined with parchment paper

Makes about 12–15 portions

Preheat the oven to 325°F.

Put the chocolate and butter in a heatproof bowl over a saucepan of simmering water (do not let the base of the bowl touch the water). Leave until melted and smooth.

Remove from the heat. Add the sugar and stir until well incorporated. Add the eggs and vanilla, stirring briskly so that you don't allow the eggs time to scramble. Don't worry if the mixture looks like it is starting to split. Add the flour, salt, and pecans and stir until well incorporated and the nuts are evenly dispersed.

Spoon the mixture into the prepared baking pan and bake in the preheated oven for about 35–40 minutes, or until golden brown and the center is still soft. Let cool completely.

chocolate icebox cake bars

A crunchy treat that requires no baking.

3 sticks plus 2 tablespoons unsalted butter

¾ cup light corn syrup

¾ cup unsweetened cocoa powder

1 lb. 11 oz. graham crackers, broken into small chunks

1⅓ cups raisins

a 13 x 9-inch baking pan, lined with parchment paper

Makes about 12–15 portions

Put the butter, corn syrup, and cocoa in a large saucepan over medium heat and heat until melted and smooth, stirring occasionally.

Put the graham cracker chunks and raisins in a large bowl and pour in the chocolate mixture. Mix with a wooden spoon until everything is well mixed and the crackers and raisins are evenly dispersed.

Press this mixture into the prepared baking pan, using a tablespoon to flatten and compress it. Cover with a sheet of parchment paper, then a tray covered in jam jars or cans to apply pressure on the cake and compress it more. Let cool completely, then refrigerate for a couple of hours, or overnight if possible.

muesli bars

These are packed with nuts, dried fruits, and cereal. You can be flexible with the ingredients, and add your favorite nuts or dried fruits.

2 sticks plus 6 tablespoons unsalted butter

1 cup light corn syrup

1 cup packed light brown sugar

2 cups rolled oats

1⅓ cups desiccated coconut

¾ cup dried apricots, finely chopped

⅓ cup dried dates, finely chopped

1¼ cups cornflakes

¾ cup sunflower seeds

½ cup dried cranberries

¾ cup shelled walnuts, chopped

¾ cup raisins

a 13 x 9-inch baking pan, lined with parchment paper

Makes about 12–15 portions

Put the butter, corn syrup, and sugar in a large saucepan over medium heat and heat until melted and smooth, stirring occasionally.

Put the oats, coconut, apricots, dates, cornflakes, sunflower seeds, cranberries, walnuts, and raisins in a large bowl and stir with a wooden spoon until everything is evenly mixed. Pour in the butter mixture and mix thoroughly until everything is well mixed and the dry ingredients are evenly dispersed.

Press this mixture into the prepared baking pan, using a tablespoon to flatten and compress it. Cover with a sheet of parchment paper, then a tray covered in jam jars or cans to apply pressure on the cake and compress it more. Let cool, then refrigerate overnight.

See photograph on page 110.

lemon bars

These bars are tangy and gooey. Dust with confectioners' sugar, and make sure the bars are chilled so that they set before slicing.

1 cup sugar

3 eggs

6 tablespoons freshly squeezed lemon juice

3 teaspoons grated lemon zest

crust

2¼ cups all-purpose flour

⅔ cup confectioners' sugar

a pinch of salt

2 sticks unsalted butter

2 teaspoons grated lemon zest

a 13 x 9-inch baking pan, lined with parchment paper

Makes about 12–15 portions

Preheat the oven to 325°F.

For the crust: Put the flour, sugar, salt, butter, and lemon zest in a freestanding electric mixer with a paddle attachment (or use a handheld electric whisk) and beat until the mixture resembles bread crumbs. Press the dough together with your hands, then press it evenly into the base of the prepared baking pan. Bake in the preheated oven for about 20 minutes, or until light golden. (Leave the oven on.) Let cool slightly.

Put the sugar, eggs, and lemon juice and zest in a bowl and whisk with a balloon whisk until well mixed. Pour carefully over the baked crust and return to the oven. Bake for 20 minutes, or until the edges are golden brown and the topping has set. Let cool completely, then cover and refrigerate overnight.

See photograph on page 111.

rocky road bars

Like the Chocolate Icebox Cake Bars on page 109, these Rocky Roads don't require baking. You can use any of your favorite chocolate bars. For cute, individual servings, scoop the mixture into muffin cases before refrigerating.

1 lb. 8 oz. milk chocolate, roughly chopped

8 regular-sized chewy chocolate bars of your choice (such as Snickers and Mars), roughly chopped

1 cup marshmallows

1¼ cups chocolate malt balls

⅔ cup dried apricots, roughly chopped

⅔ cup raisins

1 cup cornflakes

⅔ cup chocolate jimmies

a 13 x 9-inch baking pan, lined with parchment paper

Makes about 18 generous portions

Put the milk chocolate in a heatproof bowl over a saucepan of simmering water (do not let the base of the bowl touch the water). Leave until melted and smooth, stirring occasionally.

Put the chocolate bars, marshmallows, malt balls, apricots, raisins, and cornflakes in a large bowl and pour in the melted chocolate. Mix with a wooden spoon until everything is well mixed and the dry ingredients are evenly dispersed.

Press this mixture into the prepared baking pan, using a tablespoon to flatten and compress it. Sprinkle the chocolate jimmies all over the top. Let cool completely, then cover and refrigerate overnight.

muffins

ham and mushroom muffins

These savory muffins are a good breakfast treat.

3½ tablespoons butter

½ small onion, finely chopped

1 cup button mushrooms, chopped

2¾ cups all-purpose flour

2½ teaspoons baking powder

2 cups grated cheddar cheese

1 cup whole milk

1 egg

2½ oz. smoked ham, finely chopped

sea salt and freshly ground black pepper

a 12-hole muffin pan, lined with paper cases

Makes 12

Preheat the oven to 325°F.

Melt the butter in a saucepan over medium heat, then fry the onion and mushrooms until cooked. Season with sea salt and black pepper. Set aside.

Put the flour, baking powder, and cheese in a large bowl. In a separate bowl, mix the milk and egg together, then slowly pour into the flour mixture and beat with a handheld electric whisk.

Stir in the onion, mushrooms, and chopped ham with a wooden spoon until evenly dispersed.

Spoon the batter into the paper cases until two-thirds full and bake in the preheated oven for 30–35 minutes, or until deep golden and a skewer inserted in the center comes out clean. Let the muffins cool slightly in the pan before turning out onto a wire rack to cool.

carrot and zucchini muffins

Some people are surprised to hear that zucchini can be used in muffins, but they work well and give these muffins added color.

2 eggs

1 cup packed light brown sugar

⅓ cup sunflower oil

2 cups all-purpose flour

2 teaspoons baking powder

2 teaspoons ground cinnamon

⅓ cup plain yogurt

½ teaspoon pure vanilla extract

a scant cup shelled walnuts, chopped

3 carrots carrots, grated

1 zucchini, grated

a 12-hole muffin pan, lined with paper cases

Makes 12

Preheat the oven to 325°F.

Put the eggs, sugar, and oil in an electric mixer with a paddle attachment (or use a handheld electric whisk) and beat on slow speed until well combined. In a separate bowl, sift together the flour, baking powder, and cinnamon, then add to the egg mixture. Beat until just incorporated.

Add the yogurt and vanilla and mix through. Stir in the walnuts, carrots, and zucchini with a wooden spoon until evenly dispersed.

Spoon the batter into the paper cases until two-thirds full and bake in the preheated oven for 25–30 minutes, or until deep golden and a skewer inserted in the center comes out clean. Let the muffins cool slightly in the pan before turning out onto a wire rack to cool.

spinach and cheese muffins

Here's another delicious savory muffin that is always popular at the Hummingbird. Most types of hard cheese can be used, so feel free to try different varieties.

2 tablespoons butter

½ small red onion, finely chopped

2¾ cups all-purpose flour

2½ teaspoons baking powder

1 teaspoon cayenne pepper

2 cups grated cheddar cheese

1 cup whole milk

1 egg

4 oz. baby spinach leaves

*a 12-hole muffin pan,
lined with paper cases*

Makes 12

Preheat the oven to 325°F.

Melt the butter in a saucepan over medium heat, then fry the onion until cooked. Set aside.

Put the flour, baking powder, cayenne, and cheese in a large bowl. In a separate bowl, mix the milk and egg together, then slowly pour into the flour mixture and beat with a handheld electric whisk.

Stir in the onion and spinach with a wooden spoon until evenly dispersed.

Spoon the batter into the paper cases until two-thirds full and bake in the preheated oven for 30–35 minutes, or until deep golden and a skewer inserted in the center comes out clean. Let the muffins cool slightly in the pan before turning out onto a wire rack to cool.

chocolate muffins

You can vary this recipe by adding bittersweet, milk, or white chocolate chips.

2 eggs

1 cup sugar

1 cup all-purpose flour

6 tablespoons unsweetened cocoa powder

2 teaspoons baking powder

a pinch of salt

⅔ cup whole milk

¼ teaspoon pure vanilla extract

1 stick plus 3 tablespoons unsalted butter, melted

4 oz. bittersweet chocolate, roughly chopped

a 12-hole muffin pan, lined with paper cases

Makes 12

Preheat the oven to 325°F.

Put the eggs and sugar in a freestanding electric mixer with a paddle attachment (or use a handheld electric whisk) and beat until pale and well combined.

In a separate bowl, sift together the flour, cocoa, baking powder, and salt. In another bowl, combine the milk and vanilla. Gradually beat these 2 mixtures alternately into the egg mixture little by little (scrape any unmixed ingredients from the side of the bowl with a rubber spatula). Beat until just incorporated.

Stir in the melted butter with a wooden spoon, then fold in the chocolate until evenly dispersed.

Spoon the batter into the paper cases until two-thirds full and bake in the preheated oven for about 30 minutes, or until a skewer inserted in the center comes out clean. Let the muffins cool slightly in the pan before turning out onto a wire rack to cool.

blueberry muffins

The classic muffin—and the perfect start to the day with a cup of strong coffee.

2¾ cups all-purpose flour

1¾ cups sugar

1 teaspoon salt

1½ teaspoons baking powder

½ teaspoon baking soda

1½ cups buttermilk

1 egg

½ teaspoon pure vanilla extract

5 tablespoons unsalted butter, melted

1 pint blueberries

a 12-hole muffin pan,
lined with paper cases

Makes 12

Preheat the oven to 325°F.

Put the flour, sugar, salt, baking powder, and baking soda in a freestanding electric mixer with a paddle attachment (or use a handheld electric whisk) and beat on slow speed.

Put the buttermilk, egg, and vanilla into a bowl and mix to combine. Slowly pour into the flour mixture and beat until just incorporated.

Pour in the melted butter and beat until the butter has just been incorporated, then turn the mixer up to medium speed and beat until the dough is even and smooth.

Finally, gently fold in the blueberries with a wooden spoon until evenly dispersed.

Spoon the batter into the paper cases until two-thirds full and bake in the preheated oven for 20–25 minutes, or until golden and a skewer inserted in the center comes out clean. Let the muffins cool slightly in the pan before turning out onto a wire rack to cool.

banana and cinnamon muffins

Moist and sweet, nuts or chocolate chips can be added for variety.

2⅔ cups all-purpose flour

¾ teaspoon salt

1½ teaspoons baking powder

½ teaspoon baking soda

2 teaspoons ground cinnamon,
plus extra to sprinkle

¾ cup sugar, plus extra to sprinkle

1½ cups buttermilk

1 egg

½ teaspoon pure vanilla extract

5 tablespoons unsalted butter, melted

1¾ cups mashed banana

*a 12-hole muffin pan,
lined with paper cases*

Makes 12

Preheat the oven to 325°F.

Put the flour, sugar, salt, baking powder, baking soda, and cinnamon in a large bowl and beat with a handheld electric whisk until combined.

Put the buttermilk, egg, and vanilla in a bowl and mix to combine. Slowly pour into the flour mixture and beat on slow speed until just incorporated.

Pour in the melted butter and beat, then stir in the bananas with a wooden spoon until evenly dispersed.

Spoon the batter into the paper cases until two-thirds full and sprinkle a little extra sugar and cinnamon over the tops. Bake in the preheated oven for 20–30 minutes, or until golden and a skewer inserted in the center comes out clean. Let the muffins cool slightly in the pan before turning out onto a wire rack to cool.

maple and pecan muffins

Maple syrup and pecans are a classic combination, with the syrup helping to make the muffins irresistibly moist and sweet.

2⅔ cups all-purpose flour

¾ cup sugar

¾ teaspoon salt

1½ teaspoons baking powder

½ teaspoon baking soda

1½ cups buttermilk

1 egg

½ teaspoon pure vanilla extract

5 tablespoons unsalted butter, melted

1¾ cups shelled pecans, chopped, plus 12 pecan halves to decorate

¾ cup pure maple syrup

a 12-hole muffin pan, lined with paper cases

Makes 12

Preheat the oven to 325°F.

Put the flour, sugar, salt, baking powder, and baking soda in a large bowl and beat with a handheld electric whisk until combined.

Put the buttermilk, egg, and vanilla in a bowl and mix to combine. Slowly pour into the flour mixture and beat on slow speed until just incorporated.

Pour in the melted butter and beat, then stir in half the maple syrup and all the chopped pecans with a wooden spoon until evenly dispersed.

Spoon the batter into the paper cases until two-thirds full and drizzle the remaining maple syrup over the tops. Finish with a pecan half in the center of each one. Bake in the preheated oven for 20–30 minutes, or until golden and a skewer inserted in the center comes out clean. Let the muffins cool slightly in the pan before turning out onto a wire rack to cool.

cookies

double chocolate cookies

3 tablespoons unsalted butter

15 oz. bittersweet chocolate, roughly chopped

2 eggs

¾ cup plus 2 tablespoons packed light brown sugar

¼ teaspoon pure vanilla extract

⅔ cup all-purpose flour

½ teaspoon salt

½ teaspoon baking powder

a baking sheet, lined with parchment paper

Makes 12

Preheat the oven to 325°F.

Put the butter and half the chocolate in a heatproof bowl over a saucepan of simmering water (do not let the base of the bowl touch the water). Leave until melted and smooth.

Put the eggs, sugar, and vanilla in a freestanding electric mixer with a paddle attachment (or use a handheld electric whisk) and beat until well mixed. Pour in the chocolate mixture, beating on slow speed until well combined.

Sift the flour, salt, and baking powder into a separate bowl, then stir into the chocolate mixture in 3 additions, mixing well after each addition (scrape any unmixed ingredients from the side of the bowl with a rubber spatula). Finally, stir in the remaining chocolate until evenly dispersed.

Drop 12 equal amounts of cookie dough on the prepared baking sheet. Make sure that the cookies are spaced apart to allow for spreading while baking. Bake in the preheated oven for 10–15 minutes, checking regularly after 10 minutes. They are ready when the tops start to crack and look glossy. Let the cookies cool slightly on the sheet before transferring to a wire rack to cool completely.

chocolate chip cookies

1 stick plus 6 tablespoons unsalted butter, at room temperature

1¾ cups packed light brown sugar

2 eggs

½ teaspoon pure vanilla extract

3 cups all-purpose flour

½ teaspoon salt

2½ teaspoons baking soda

8 oz. chocolate chips, roughly chopped

2 baking sheets, lined with parchment paper

Makes 24

Preheat the oven to 325°F.

Put the butter and sugar in a freestanding electric mixer with a paddle attachment (or use a handheld electric whisk) and cream until light and fluffy. Add the eggs one at a time, mixing well and scraping any unmixed ingredients from the side of the bowl with a rubber spatula after each addition. Turn the mixer down to slow speed and beat in the vanilla.

Add the flour, salt, and baking soda and mix well until a smooth dough is formed. Stir in the chocolate chips until evenly dispersed.

Drop 12 equal amounts of cookie dough on each prepared baking sheet. Make sure that the cookies are spaced apart to allow for spreading while baking. Bake in the preheated oven for about 10 minutes, or until golden brown around the edges and quite flat. Let the cookies cool slightly on the sheets before transferring to a wire rack to cool completely. The cookies should be soft and chewy.

peanut butter cookies

These are an all-time American favorite—and whether you put chocolate chips in or not is up to you! We use crunchy peanut butter for a better texture and flavor.

1 stick plus 6 tablespoons unsalted butter, at room temperature

1 cup sugar

1 cup packed light brown sugar

2 eggs

½ teaspoon pure vanilla extract

1 cup crunchy peanut butter

2⅔ cups all-purpose flour

2½ teaspoons baking soda

½ teaspoon salt

½ cup chocolate chips, chopped

*2 baking sheets,
lined with parchment paper*

Makes 24

Preheat the oven to 325°F.

Put the butter and sugars in a freestanding electric mixer with a paddle attachment (or use a handheld electric whisk) and cream until light and fluffy. Add the eggs one at a time, mixing well and scraping any unmixed ingredients from the side of the bowl with a rubber spatula after each addition. Turn the mixer down to slow speed and beat in the vanilla and peanut butter.

Add the flour, baking soda, and salt and mix well until a smooth dough is formed. Stir in the chocolate chips until evenly dispersed.

Drop 12 equal amounts of cookie dough on each prepared baking sheet. Make sure that the cookies are spaced apart to allow for spreading while baking. Bake in the preheated oven for about 10 minutes, or until golden brown around the edges and quite flat. Let the cookies cool slightly on the sheets before transferring to a wire rack to cool completely. The cookies should be soft and chewy.

white chocolate and pecan cookies

This is a flavor combination that works very well to create a more sophisticated cookie. Bittersweet or milk chocolate can be substituted if you don't like white chocolate.

2 sticks unsalted butter,
at room temperature

½ cup sugar

1 cup packed light brown sugar

2 eggs

½ teaspoon pure vanilla extract

3 cups all-purpose flour

½ teaspoon salt

¼ teaspoon baking powder

3½ oz. white chocolate, chopped

⅔ cup shelled pecans, chopped

2 baking sheets,
lined with parchment paper

Makes 24

Put the butter and sugars in a freestanding electric mixer with a paddle attachment (or use a handheld electric whisk) and cream until light and fluffy. Add the eggs one at a time, mixing well and scraping any unmixed ingredients from the side of the bowl with a rubber spatula after each addition. Turn the mixer down to slow speed and beat in the vanilla.

Add the flour, salt, and baking powder and mix well until a smooth dough is formed. Stir in the chocolate and pecans until evenly dispersed.

Divide the dough in half and shape each half into 2 equal rolls about 6–7 inches in length. Wrap the rolls in plastic wrap and put them in the freezer to set completely for a couple of hours.

Preheat the oven to 325°F.

Remove the plastic wrap and cut the dough into disks about 1 inch thick. Arrange the cookies on the prepared baking sheets. Make sure that the cookies are spaced apart to allow for spreading while baking. Bake in the preheated oven for 10–15 minutes, or until golden around the edges and quite flat. Let the cookies cool slightly on the sheets before transferring to a wire rack to cool completely. The cookies should be soft and chewy.

oatmeal raisin cookies

Here's a lovely, cinnamony cookie made with wholesome rolled oats.

2 sticks plus 2 tablespoons unsalted butter, at room temperature

¾ cup sugar

¾ cup packed dark brown sugar

2 eggs

¼ teaspoon pure vanilla extract

2¾ cups all-purpose flour

1 teaspoon salt

1 teaspoon baking soda

½ teaspoon ground cinnamon

1 cup rolled oats

1⅓ cups raisins

*2 baking sheets,
lined with parchment paper*

Makes 20

Preheat the oven to 325°F.

Put the butter and sugars in a freestanding electric mixer with a paddle attachment (or use a handheld electric whisk) and cream until light and fluffy. Add the eggs one at a time, mixing well and scraping any unmixed ingredients from the side of the bowl with a rubber spatula after each addition. Turn the mixer down to slow speed and beat in the vanilla.

Sift together the flour, salt, baking soda, and cinnamon in a separate bowl, add the oats, and mix well. Add to the butter mixture and beat until well mixed. Stir in the raisins with a wooden spoon until evenly dispersed.

Drop equal amounts of cookie dough on the prepared baking sheets. Make sure that the cookies are spaced apart to allow for spreading while baking. Bake in the preheated oven for about 12 minutes, or until golden and firm. Check them regularly to make sure they are not burning. When you are happy that they are cooked through, remove from the oven and let cool slightly on the sheets before transferring to a wire rack to cool completely.

sugar cookies

This recipe forms the base for all our holiday cookies. Roll it out and use shaped cookie cutters to make your own festive cookies.

1 stick plus 6 tablespoons unsalted butter, at room temperature

1⅓ cups sugar

¼ teaspoon pure vanilla extract

1 egg

3 cups all-purpose flour

a pinch of salt

½ teaspoon cream of tartar

Royal Icing (page 140)

shaped cookie cutters
2 baking sheets,
lined with parchment paper

Makes about 20

Preheat the oven to 325°F.

Put the butter, sugar, and vanilla in a freestanding electric mixer with a paddle attachment (or use a handheld electric whisk) and cream until light and fluffy. Add the egg and mix well, scraping any unmixed ingredients from the side of the bowl with a rubber spatula.

Add the flour, salt, and cream of tartar and mix well, but don't overmix. The dough should be light, soft, and easy to handle.

Lightly dust a clean work surface with flour and roll out the dough with a rolling pin. Cut out shapes with your choice of cookie cutters. Arrange the cookies on the prepared baking sheets and bake in the preheated oven for about 10 minutes. Check them regularly to make sure they are not burning. The cookies should be very light golden on the outer edges and paler in the center. When you are happy that they are cooked through, remove from the oven and let cool slightly on the sheets before transferring to a wire rack to cool completely. Decorate with Royal Icing.

gingerbread men

You don't have to use a gingerbread man cutter with this recipe, but it's so much fun to decorate each one individually! Leaving the dough to rest overnight makes the cookies better the next day.

3 cups all-purpose flour

¾ teaspoon baking soda

2 teaspoons ground ginger

2 teaspoons ground cinnamon

½ teaspoon ground allspice

¼ teaspoon ground nutmeg

½ teaspoon salt

1½ sticks unsalted butter,
at room temperature

⅔ cups packed dark brown sugar

1 egg

½ cup dark molasses

royal icing

1 egg white

½ teaspoon freshly squeezed
lemon juice

2½ cups confectioners' sugar, sifted

food coloring, optional

gingerbread cookie cutters
2 baking sheets,
lined with parchment paper

Makes about 24

Sift together the flour, baking soda, ginger, cinnamon, allspice, nutmeg, and salt in a large bowl and set aside.

Put the butter and sugars in a freestanding electric mixer with a paddle attachment (or use a handheld electric whisk) and cream on slow speed until light and fluffy. Turn the mixer up to medium speed and beat in the egg and molasses, scraping any unmixed ingredients from the side of the bowl with a rubber spatula.

Turn the mixer back down to slow speed and slowly add the flour mixture a couple of tablespoons at a time, stopping often to scrape any unmixed ingredients from the side of the bowl with a rubber spatula. Once an even dough has formed, take it out of the mixer, divide into 3, and wrap each piece in plastic wrap. Chill overnight in the fridge.

When you are ready to bake the cookies, preheat the oven to 325°F.

Take the dough out of the fridge and let soften for about 10 minutes. Lightly dust a clean work surface with flour and roll out the dough to a thickness of about ¼ inch with a rolling pin. Cut out shapes with the cookie cutters. Arrange the cookies on the prepared baking sheets and bake in the preheated oven for about 10–15 minutes. Let the cookies cool slightly on the sheets before turning out onto a wire rack to cool completely.

For the royal icing: Beat the egg white and lemon juice together in a freestanding electric mixer with a paddle attachment (or use a handheld electric whisk). Gradually start adding the confectioners' sugar, mixing well after each addition to ensure all sugar is incorporated. Whisk until you get stiff peaks. If the icing is too runny, add a little more sugar. Stir in a couple of drops of food coloring, if using, and decorate the cookies.

index

conversion chart

Volume equivalents:

American	Metric	Imperial
6 tbsp butter	85 g	3 oz.
7 tbsp butter	100 g	3½ oz.
1 stick butter	115 g	4 oz.
1 teaspoon	5 ml	
1 tablespoon	15 ml	
¼ cup	60 ml	2 fl.oz.
⅓ cup	75 ml	2½ fl.oz.
½ cup	125 ml	4 fl.oz.
⅔ cup	150 ml	5 fl.oz. (¼ pint)
¾ cup	175 ml	6 fl.oz.
1 cup	250 ml	8 fl.oz.

Oven temperatures:

170°C	(325°F)	Gas 3
180°C	(350°F)	Gas 4
190°C	(375°F)	Gas 5
200°C	(400°F)	Gas 6
220°C	(425°F)	Gas 8

Weight equivalents:

Imperial	Metric
1 oz.	30 g
2 oz.	55 g
3 oz.	85 g
3½ oz.	100 g
4 oz.	115 g
5 oz.	140 g
6 oz.	175 g
8 oz. (½ lb.)	225 g
9 oz.	250 g
10 oz.	280 g
11½ oz.	325 g
12 oz.	350 g
13 oz.	375 g
14 oz.	400 g
15 oz.	425 g
16 oz. (1 lb.)	450 g

Measurements:

Inches	Cm
¼ inch	0.5 cm
½ inch	1 cm
¾ inch	1.5 cm
1 inch	2.5 cm
2 inches	5 cm
3 inches	7 cm
4 inches	10 cm
5 inches	12 cm
6 inches	15 cm
7 inches	18 cm
8 inches	20 cm
9 inches	23 cm
10 inches	25 cm
11 inches	28 cm
12 inches	30 cm

author's acknowledgments

With thanks to all the Hummingbird Bakery chefs that have devised our recipes over the years, including: Joanne Adams, Jhanet Thyssen, and Barbara Bachota. A very special thank you to Heath MacIntyre for her very hard and excellent work in sorting through all the recipes, writing them out, testing them, and adapting them to make them work in a home-baking environment! Thanks to Steve Painter, Peter Cassidy, Bridget Sargeson, Céline Hughes, Alison Starling, and all the team at Ryland Peters & Small for producing such a beautiful and special book. Finally, a big thank you to all the staff, past and present, that have made The Hummingbird Bakery such a success.

publisher's acknowledgments

Thanks to the following for the kind loan of props for this book:

Something...
58 Lamb's Conduit Street
Bloomsbury
London WC1N 3LW
United Kingdom
www.something-shop.com

Jane Wicks, Kitchenalia
'Country Ways'
Strand Quay
Rye
East Sussex
United Kingdom